THE
UNKNOWN
PUCCINI

Courtesy of the Library of Congress.

The Unknown
PUCCINI

A historical perspective on the songs,
including little-known music
from *Edgar* and *La Rondine*,
with complete music for voice and piano

MICHAEL KAYE

New York   Oxford
OXFORD UNIVERSITY PRESS
1987

Oxford University Press

Oxford   New York   Toronto
Delhi   Bombay   Calcutta   Madras   Karachi
Petaling Jaya   Singapore   Hong Kong   Tokyo
Nairobi   Dar es Salaam   Cape Town
Melbourne   Auckland

and associated companies in
Beirut   Berlin   Ibadan   Nicosia

Published by Oxford University Press, Inc.,
200 Madison Avenue, New York, New York 10016

Oxford is a registered trademark of Oxford University Press

Library of Congress Cataloging-in-Publication Data

Puccini, Giacomo, 1858–1924.
The unknown Puccini.

Principally Italian works, also printed as text
with English translation preceding each work.
Includes critical commentaries.
Bibliography: p.
Includes indexes.
Contents: Part 1. Songs: A te ; Vexilla Regis prodeunt
etc. — Part 2. Music originally included in stage
works etc.
1. Songs with piano.   2. Operas—Excerpts—Vocal
scores with piano.   I. Kaye, Michael.   II. Title.
M3.1.P85V64   1986   85-755330
ISBN 0-19-385745-6

9 8 7 6 5 4 3 2 1

Printed in the United States of America
on acid free paper

Giacomo Puccini è un conquistatore di moltitudini. Oltre i monti, le fiumane, gli oceani, per le città fragorose e per i paesi di terre selvagge, nei teatri di pietra e d'oro della ricchezza, e fra le tende dei minatori nomadi, ha portato come un vessillo spiegato al vento in giornate di vittoria, il tricolore d'Italia, il nome d'Italia, la divina melodia d'Italia. È dovere onorare questo fratel nostro maggiore e migliore, e per rendergli onore conviene conoscerlo, conviene amarlo.

Fausto Salvatori

Meno *bataclan* faranno intorno alla mia persona più grato mi avrano.

Giacomo Puccini

Foreword

No one—least of all the composer—would claim that Puccini's songs are major works. As he was fond of saying, his talent lay exclusively in the theater. But anything written by a major composer is of interest, even a minor piece. Puccini's songs and his other rare nonoperatic works tell us something about him, about his life, and also about his mind.

For one thing, he was musically parsimonious. If he used a good tune in a song (as he did in *Sole e amore*), it tends to crop up later in a stage work. For another thing, like many shy and reserved people, Puccini was a good friend. His friends were not many—they tended also to be Tuscan neighbors—but to the select few, he opened his heart, as we know from his letters. And often a Puccini song is also a pledge of friendship: *Avanti Urania!*, written for the launching of the boat of his hunting companion the Marchese Carlo Ginori-Lisci; or the delicate lullaby for the infant Memmo Lippi, born shortly after the death of his father, another of Puccini's Lucca friends.

The songs were never written in groups; each has its own specific source. And they were almost never written without an occasion. Sometimes these occasions were private, sometimes they were public. And one—which elicited, not without problems, the *Inno a Roma*—was a state event, attended by members of the royal family.

In the past Puccini's biographers—and even his bibliographer Cecil Hopkinson—have tended to neglect these works, and many errors crept into the descriptions of them. Titles were mentioned incorrectly (one song was given two titles, then sometimes mentioned as two different works). A song by a Russian princess was for many years erroneously attributed to Puccini.

With single-minded devotion, Michael Kaye has unraveled all these tangled webs, cleared up the murky parts of the story, and made the songs readily available to scholars and singers (who may find them a welcome addition to the sparse Italian section of the recital repertory). Kaye's edition of these pieces has involved immense amounts of musicological detection, and even the nonspecialist will enjoy his accounts of the origins and histories of the songs. Indirectly, their story is also the story of Puccini himself and of his career. It is no accident that, among the authors of the texts he set, we find figures like Antonio Ghislanzoni, Luigi Illica, and Giuseppe Adami—all of them important characters in the world of Italian opera during the late years of the nineteenth century and the early years of the twentieth. And it is significant that among Puccini's poets there is Puccini himself, for he enjoyed writing verses, often foolish doggerel for the delight of his friends, but occasionally he revealed a more serious, melancholy vein, the same vein that runs through some of the songs, culminating in the haunting, enigmatic *Morire?*, composed during the first world war, in a time of great dejection.

We know how much autobiography there is in Puccini's work, from the ebullience of his Bohemians derived from his own carefree student days in Milan, to the cloister of *Suor Angelica* based on the convent where one of the composer's sisters had retired from the world. The songs are often doubly autobiographical—first, as has been said, because they refer to specific events; and second, because they may also reflect a general mood, a time, brief or extended, in the composer's private life.

Minor works, as we have agreed, but never trivial and—as can be said of virtually every note by Puccini—never lifeless, never dull.

William Weaver

Acknowledgments

I would be remiss if I did not acknowledge the musicological detective work on the subject of Puccini's nonoperatic works already done by Mario Morini and the late Cecil Hopkinson. Their informative writings aroused my curiosity, which led me to this undertaking. I am very grateful to many people who facilitated my research and helped in the preparation of this volume. I would particularly like to express my thanks to the following individuals, librarians, and institutions: Prof. Piergiuseppe Bozzetti, Cultural Attaché of the Italian Embassy in Washington, D.C.; J. Rigbie Turner and The Pierpont Morgan Library; Frederick R. Koch, New York City; Louise Goldberg, Ross Wood, and the Sibley Music Library of the Eastman School of Music; Charles Niles and the Mugar Memorial Library at Boston University; Betty Arnold and the Pennsylvania State University Library; Kent State University Library; Maestro Herbert Handt, Lucca; the Istituto Musicale Parregiato "L. Boccherini," Lucca; the Conservatorio Giuseppe Verdi, Milan; Elisabeth Auman and the staff of the Music Division of the Library of Congress, especially Elmer Booze, Gail Freunsch, Charles Sens, and Wayne Shirley; Samuel Brylawski of the Recorded Sound Reference Center at the Library of Congress; Ruth Edge and the EMI Archives, London; Barbara Bodine, New York City; Dr. Karl Eibenschütz, London; John Gualiani, Milan; Thomas Hetrick, Baltimore; the late Robert Holton (who was instrumental in arranging for the permissions required in order to publish the *Inno a Roma* and the excerpts from *La Rondine*); Casa Musicale Sonzogno di Piero Ostali, Milan; Marion v. Hartlieb and Universal Edition AG, Vienna; Richard Macnutt, Tunbridge Wells; Maestro Raffaele Mingardo, Teatro alla Scala; Maestro Antonio de Almeida, Saint-Rémy-de-Provence; Martin Schlumpf, Munich; Anne Stovall-Charrier, Potomac, Maryland; and Kathy Janeczek, Washington, D.C. I also received generous assistance from opera historian Charles Jahant of Hyattsville, Maryland, whose important annals of operatic performance and unique knowledge of opera singers were invaluable resources.

I am indebted to Puccini biographer Howard Greenfeld for kindly allowing me access to rare Pucciniana in his library, and to his wife, Paola A. Greenfeld, who helped me decipher several of the composer's letters and other documents.

An invitation to write an article about Puccini's songs for *The Opera Quarterly* brought about a fortuitous meeting with the editors of that publication, Irene and Sherwin Sloan, of Woodland Hills, California. Irene accepted the difficult task of editing my text for this book. I am very grateful to her for her unflagging patience, careful attention to detail, and numerous helpful suggestions; many improvements in the text are the result of her splendid talents as an editor.

I would also like to thank William Weaver for reading a very early draft of this book and for writing the foreword.

Michael Kaye
Washington, D.C.

Contents

PART ONE: Songs of Puccini

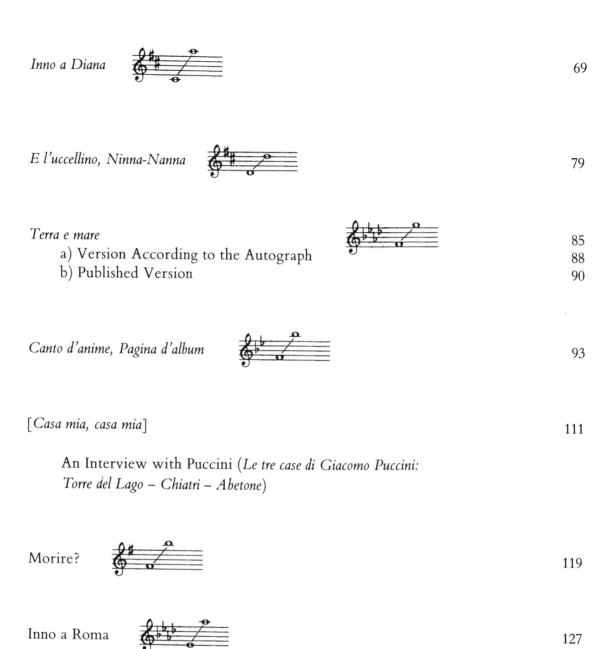
PART TWO: Music Originally Included in Stage Works

Introduction

> Poor Vamba! I feel a little guilty for not having set that Hymn to the Cricket
> of his to music – it was my reluctance to write small pieces – I tried to write
> it, but after only a few notes I stopped abruptly - It is still on my piano stand.[1]

THE SONGS OF GIACOMO PUCCINI are a means to better understanding the man and his music. Throughout his career, Puccini was hesitant to write music that was not connected with the theater, where he knew that his creative genius could best be heard.

> I have never written a *Lied* or a *romance*. I need the great window of the
> stage—There I am at ease. . . . When traveling I cannot see a landscape or
> hear a word without thinking of a possible dramatic situation.[2]

> What could I have done if I didn't get lucky with my operas? Teach? What?
> How could I if I don't know anything? Play the organ? With my clumsy
> hands? Band director? I am so authoritarian that the musicians would have
> ended that by playing the drum on my tummy! By now I would have been
> dead with misery and pains, especially from the latter because of the morbid
> sensitivity that has always dominated me.[3]

He was not interested in exploring the subtleties of song composition in the manner of a Fauré, Debussy, or Richard Strauss (although their music interested him), but he did write beautiful songs for voice and piano. Some were required student works; others were salon songs first published in now-defunct periodicals, as musical supplements to well-known magazines or as "special editions." Italian publishers liked to designate these special editions as a *numero unico*, which they would offer as a bonus to subscribers, or issue in honor of specific events. The songs dating from his most prolific years, the period of *La Bohème*, *Tosca*, and *Madama Butterfly* (1896–1904), were written for friends. *Canto d'anime* was composed expressly for the gramophone. In *E l'uccellino* and *Terra e mare*, Puccini approached the refinement of an accomplished song composer, but all of his songs reflect the stages of development of his very personal musical language.

The songs in this collection date from disparate periods in the composer's life: sacred and secular juvenilia written between 1875 and 1880 in Lucca; student compositions and works written in Milan between 1880 and 1884, prior to the première of *Le Villi*; occasional pieces dedicated to friends written between 1888 and 1899, after he achieved his first major operatic successes; and mature works written at Torre del Lago from 1902 to 1919. His *Requiem*, composed in memory of Giuseppe Verdi in 1905, and the *Inno a Roma* (1919), originally written for voice and piano, but better known in arrangements for multiple voices and instruments, are also discussed, as are the incomplete, fragmentary, or missing works, from which I have quoted thematic material. The existence of these potential additions to the vocal repertoire may come as a surprise to many people. Most of Puccini's nonoperatic vocal works are known only to scholars and aficionados of Pucciniana—and then often only by title.

---

1. Letter to Carlo Paladini dated 26 November 1920 in Carlo Paladini, *Giacomo Puccini* (Florence: Vallecchi Editore, 1961). Vamba (Luigi Bertelli), one of Puccini's Lucchese friends, died the day after Puccini wrote this letter.
2. Quoted by Michel Georges-Michel in *Un demi-siècle de gloires théâtrales* (Paris: André Bonne, 1950).
3. Letter to Carlo Paladini dated 26 November 1920 in Paladini, *Giacomo Puccini*, pp. 150–51.

While researching material for this book in the United States and in Europe, I observed numerous bits of erroneous and confusing information that have generally been accepted as true by the composer's major biographers and commentators. The most prevalent example of misinformation concerns the titles by which the songs are known. First lines of the texts have been incorrectly cited as titles. Alternate versions of the same work have been incorrectly catalogued as separate entries. The titles as they appear on some of the manuscripts are different from those that were eventually assigned to the first published editions. Inaccurate attributions of authorship have also been made. (The song entitled *Ditele*, which the majority of discographies ascribe to Puccini, is not by Puccini at all.)[4] Authorship of some of the song texts has also been erroneously cited. For example, Carlo Abeniacar, an author, a photojournalist, a friend of Puccini's, and a fellow hunter, wrote the poem for Puccini's *Inno a Diana*, a song that has nothing whatsoever to do with the *Inno a Roma*, for which the Roman poet and playwright Fausto Salvatori supplied the text. It is not uncommon to read in literature about Puccini that Salvatori (or Salvadori [*sic*]) was Abeniacar's pseudonym, or that Puccini wrote the texts for *Storiella d'amore* and "Salve del ciel Regina" [*sic*]. There are also a surprising number of inconsistencies in dating the songs in various catalogues of Puccini's works.[5] Although the instrumental works are not in the scope of this volume, it is interesting to note that "a very brilliant little march" ("una marcetta brillantissima"),[6] *Scossa elettrica*, originally for piano—believed to be unpublished—was, in fact, engraved by G. Ricordi & Co. and published in *I Telegrafisti a Volta* (Como: Tipografia Pietro Cairoli, 1899). This *numero unico* honored Alessandro Volta, the inventor of the battery, on the occasion of the 1899 Esposizione di Como and the World Congress of Telegraphers. Its publication was announced in the *Gazzetta Musicale di Milano* of 17 August 1899. The signed but undated manuscript is owned by Richard Macnutt, Tunbridge Wells, England. It is complete on two pages (82 measures, E major, $\frac{2}{4}$, A-B-A-C-A form, plus 8 repeated measures and a Da Capo); the manuscript includes 24 measures of two other, seemingly unrelated, themes:

---

4. See Appendix II.

5. Following the chronological list of songs found on page xix is an alphabetical list of the titles as they appear in various references cited in the Bibliography and elsewhere in the text. Duplicate and/or erroneous titles for single works are included so that the reader can perceive at a glance the extent of the variations by which Puccini's songs have been catalogued.

6. Quoted in the *Gazzetta Musicale di Milano*, 17 August 1899, pp. 410–11.

Judging from the character of the music and the presence of certain unpianistic entrances of phrases in counterpoint, it seems likely that it was transcribed for concert band and performed at the Como exposition.[7] These are only some examples of information which, in the interest of a more accurate perspective on Puccini's nonoperatic vocal and instrumental works, should be better known.

AUTOGRAPHS AND MANUSCRIPTS: Many of Puccini's smaller compositions survive only in preliminary sketches or as incomplete rough-draft scores. The locations of most of the manuscripts are known. Some of their owners and/or custodians have changed since the publication of Hopkinson's bibliography.[8] The large collection of manuscripts given by Puccini to the Istituto Musicale Luigi Boccherini in 1901 are, according to the librarian, Giulio Battelli, currently in the possession of the Fondazione Puccini di Lucca, and at the time of this writing it has not been determined if they will be returned to the Boccherini Institute. Other manuscripts appear to have vanished from their previously known (or surmised) repositories: as of 1983, the library of the Milan Conservatory was unable to locate the autographs of *Melanconia* and the *Solfeggi* for voice and piano. I have traced others to The Pierpont Morgan Library (*Inno a Diana*, [*Casa mia, casa mia*], interesting scores of *Le Villi, La fanciulla del West*, and sections of *Edgar, La Bohème,* and *Madama Butterfly*), the Sibley Library of the Eastman School of Music, the Mugar Library at Boston University (*Avanti Urania!*), and to important autograph dealers.[9] A presentation copy of the manuscript of *E l'uccellino* and an unpublished *romanza* entitled *Ah! se potesse* are suspected to exist in private collections. The locations of the manuscripts of *Canto d'anime* and *Morire?* remain unknown.

MUSIC AND EDITORIAL PRACTICE: The songs have been arranged in chronological order in their original keys. In those pieces for which manuscripts (or photocopies of the manuscripts) were available, Puccini's autograph indications for tempo, phrasing (even if appearing somewhat unorthodox by modern editorial practice), dynamics, and certainly the musical and literary texts have been preserved. If an original manuscript (or photocopy) was not available, then first editions and subsequent printings issued in Puccini's lifetime have served as the sources for the present edition.

Abbreviations for tempo indications have been spelled out; for example, And^te = Andante.

Autograph instructions and shorthand devices for indicating repetitions have been realized in accordance with modern conventions. Positions of hairpins, tempo indicators, and accent marks have been likewise normalized.

Regular slurs indicate what appears in the principal source. Some of these slurs have been extended; for example, where Puccini stopped in the middle of a word. Dotted slurs signify a possible interpretation.

Pointed brackets < > are used to differentiate additions from other autograph sources.

---

7. See also Giorgio Magri, *Puccini e le sue rime* (Milan: Giorgio Borletti Editore, 1974), p. 329.

8. Cecil Hopkinson, *A Bibliography of the Works of Giacomo Puccini: 1858–1924* (New York: Broude Brothers Limited, 1968).

9. I have observed that some of Puccini's letters previously known only in translations published in books by, among others, del Fiorentino, Marek, and Seligman (see the Bibliography beginning on page 231) have recently been offered for sale by various autograph dealers in New York City.

Parentheses ( ) are used to specify information originating from a qualified secondary source—usually the first published edition issued in Puccini's lifetime. Obvious typographical errors have been corrected without comment.

Editorial additions appear in square brackets [ ].

When no initial dynamic level is supplied, Puccini probably expected that the singer would choose one appropriate to the character of the text and the musical setting.

Throughout the text, the song titles are set in italics.

TEXTS AND TRANSLATIONS: Whenever possible, the literary texts have been collated with the originals. Variants between the manuscripts of the songs and the published versions of the texts in other sources are indicated in the music. Each song is preceded by the Italian verses and a nonsinging English translation, which is intended not as poetry but as an aid to performers' understanding. These translations are my own. In the commentary preceding each song, I have endeavored to provide a significant amount of material in Puccini's own words selected from his correspondence and other important resource material. These translations are also my own, with the exception of a few excerpts (published only in translation) for which the original Italian was not available. Sources for the quotations are cited in footnotes throughout the text. In most cases, the original editors of these letters have retained Puccini's strange punctuation (or absence thereof). I have done likewise in documents published herein for the first time. In the translations, however, I have taken the liberty of supplying a few editorial additions and some manipulations of punctuation.

Puccini often reused sections of his songs in his operas. According to Arnaldo Fraccaroli, one of the composer's first biographers, of his self-borrowings Puccini reportedly said: "After all, let us speak the truth, where is the theft? I robbed myself. Am I then a thief? I would be the victim too."[10] Although not profound in terms of yielding a deeper understanding of Puccini's working methods, these self-borrowings are often fascinating. Some of the more important examples occur in *Manon Lescaut*, in which the recitative and aria "Mentìa l'avviso," for tenor and piano, written in 1883 as part of his final examinations at the Milan Conservatory, became des Grieux's famous "Donna non vidi mai." In *La Bohème*, the song *Sole e amore* of 1888 was used as the basis for the quartet that closes Act III. In *Tosca* and *Madama Butterfly*, one hears echoes of the songs *Avanti Urania!* and *Inno a Diana*. In *Gianni Schicchi*, the *Canto d'anime* of 1904 served as the prototype for Rinuccio's "Firenze è come un albero fiorito." *Morire?* also served double duty as Puccini and Adami's contribution to an album of music sold to benefit the Italian Red Cross and as an entrance aria for Ruggero in the second version of *La Rondine*.

There are numerous other examples of Puccini's turning to his songs (as well as to his instrumental works) for source material for his operas. It was not that he was at a loss for melodic inspiration. He probably wanted to hear those sections he chose to borrow from himself blossom in the theater, where the beauty of the music he had previously written and the orchestrations he could create for them would enhance them in even more expressive settings.

Although Puccini did not write an abundance of music in smaller forms, he was certainly a prolific letter writer. In addition to his copious business correspondence he did not hesitate to put

---

10. Arnaldo Fraccaroli, *La vita di Giacomo Puccini* (Milan: Ricordi, 1958).

pen to paper to tell a friend about his hunting plans, his travel itinerary, to suggest a revision in a certain scene written by one of his librettists, or to share one of his own poems with a friend or relative. Sometimes his letters took the form of a few notes of music:

On at least one occasion he composed a letter in the form of a complete melody, as was the case with the following message (written much earlier) to the conductor Leopoldo Mugnone:[11]

---

11. The manuscript of this letter is in the possession of the Istituto di Studi Verdiani in Parma.

ci sa - lu - ta - sti tu! Il sot - to scrit - to au -

to - re, [*sic*] El - vi - ra e Fos - chet - ti - na,

rallentando

la se - ra e la mat - ti - na, ba - ci t'in-via -no e fior

Milan, 20.5. [18]96
Via Solferino 27

Hail Maria Leopolda, [*sic*] we salute you with a chorus
The way you greeted us from atop the deck!
The undersigned author, Elvira and little Fosca,
Night and day, send kisses and flowers to you.

G. Puccini

The first part of this volume is as complete a collection of Puccini's nonoperatic songs as was possible to assemble. The songs are not restricted to one voice category but are appropriate for different vocal ranges, both male and female. Because it is hoped that this volume will be useful to sopranos, mezzo-sopranos, tenors, baritones, and basses, I could not resist the temptation to include a section of virtually unknown music that Puccini wrote for various voices. The second part is therefore comprised of excerpts from two rarely performed operas, *Edgar* and *La Rondine*, the latter that hybrid combining the world of operetta and lyric opera. The collection also features the first publications of the early song entitled *A te*, Puccini's setting of the "Vexilla Regis prodeunt" commissioned for the small church in Bagni di Lucca around 1875, and a very brief song, [*Casa mia, casa mia*]. For no other reason than that they delighted me, I included an interview with the maestro himself, in which he describes his houses at Torre del Lago, Chiatri, and Abetone, as well as a favorite recipe for coots as prepared in his kitchen.

I hope that one day we may benefit from a critical edition of all of Puccini's works and from a comprehensive publication of his correspondence—neither of which is currently available.[12] One always has hopes of unearthing a previously unpublished manuscript of a great composer. There may still be unknown songs, compositions, and manuscripts of Puccini in jealously guarded private collections that may surface and supplement our knowledge and our enjoyment of Puccini's music. Until then, I hope that this collection will serve insofar as the nonoperatic vocal works are concerned.

---

12. Annotated scores of *La Bohème*, *Tosca*, and *Madama Butterfly* that include information previously found only in holograph material and other important primary sources have been issued by Ricordi in Italy and Germany. Such publications ought to be better known in the United States, but, as of this writing, they are not the performing editions widely used by opera companies, those generally studied, or even those readily available.

Chronological List of Puccini's Songs

Whenever possible, the dates represent the year
of composition, not that of the first publication.

TITLE	DATE	TEXT	COMPOSED AT
A te	1875 (?)	?	Lucca
Vexilla [Regis prodeunt] a 2 Voci	1878 (?)	Venantius Honorius Clementianus Fortunatus	"
Melanconia	1881 (?)	Antonio Ghislanzoni	Milan
Salve Regina	1882 (?)	Antonio Ghislanzoni	"
Ah! se potesse	1882 (?)	?	Lucca
Ad una morta!	1882 (?)	Antonio Ghislanzoni	"
"Mentìa l'avviso"	1883	Felice Romani	"
Storiella d'amore	1883	Antonio Ghislanzoni	"
Sole e amore	1888	Giacomo Puccini (?)	"
Solfeggi	1888	—	Milan
Avanti *Urania*!	1896	Renato Fucini	Torre del Lago
Inno a Diana	1897	Carlo Abeniacar	"
E l'uccellino	1899	Renato Fucini	"
Terra e mare	1902	Enrico Panzacchi	"
Canto d'anime	1904	Luigi Illica	"
[Casa mia, casa mia]	1908	Giacomo Puccini	"
Morire?	1917 (?)[1]	Giuseppe Adami	"
Inno a Roma	1919	Fausto Salvatori	"

---

1. The exact year of composition is unknown; it was certainly published for the first time ca. 1917–1918.

List of Titles
by Which the Songs Are Known

PART I

Songs of Puccini

A TE

Authorship of text uncertain

A TE is one of the longest of Puccini's songs, yet the least is known about its origins. Obviously an early composition, it probably dates from Puccini's student years at the Pacini Institute—now known as the Istituto Musicale Pareggiato "L. Boccherini"—in his native city of Lucca, where he studied composition with Carlo Angeloni.[1]

It may have been composed as a required student work. The title is uncertain, for in the autograph manuscript Puccini drew a line through the words "a te," which are written above the music. The undated six-page manuscript was among those given by the composer to the Boccherini Institute in 1901. Written in a very early hand, the song is complete on five pages. The first fourteen measures of the voice part are written again on page six. Judging from the numerous cross-outs, changes, ink smudges, and careless errors in notation—particularly in the accompaniment—this manuscript was probably Puccini's working copy of the score, not one intended for performance.

In various catalogues of the composer's works, some compilers have erroneously transcribed the first line of text as "O quanto è vano." Authorship of the text has been attributed to a poet named Romano—possibly resulting from a reading of a word that Puccini wrote, but also crossed out, after the indication "a te." I have been unable to decipher that word. It may actually be "Romanza," followed by three undecipherable letters; then in miniature: "$\wp$."

Dubious title and poet notwithstanding, the present edition is faithful to the manuscript and, to the best of my knowledge, this is its first publication.

---

1. Angeloni (b. Lucca, 16 July 1834; d. there, 13 January 1901) had been a pupil of Puccini's father, Michele Puccini (b. 27 November 1813; d. 18 February 1864), who had studied with Mercadante and Donizetti.

A TE

Ho! quant'io t'amo,
O quanto in me forte è il desio,
Di stringerti al cuor mio,
Di farti palpitar.

Da te così lontano
Io soffro, io soffro assai;
Né pace io trovo mai
Perchè troppo è l'amore,
Troppo è l'amor!

O mia vittoria, O mio tesoro,
O bene mio, O mio sol pensiero,
E dammi un bacio e il mondo intiero,
E mi farai tutto obbliar.

O mia vittoria, O mio tesor sara,
O bene mio, O mio sol pensiero,
E dammi un bacio e il mondo intiero,
E mi farai tosto obbliar!

TO YOU

Oh, how very much I love you!
How strong is the desire in me
To hold you tightly to my heart,
To fill you with excitement.

When I am so far away from you
I suffer, I suffer so much;
Nor do I ever find peace
Because my love for you is so strong,
Love is too strong!

O my victory, my darling,
My beloved, my one and only thought,
Give me a kiss and that will make me
Forget everything!

O my victory, you will be my treasure,
My beloved, my one and only thought;
Give me a kiss and that will make me
Quickly forget the entire world!

4

A TE

First Edition

Authorship of
text uncertain

Music by
GIACOMO PUCCINI

Edited by Michael Kaye

Ho! quant' io t'a - mo, o

---

* Puccini originally wrote "Adagio," but crossed it out and substituted "Andante."

quan - to in me for-te è il de - si - o,
for - te è il de - si - o, di strin - ger ti al cuor
mi - o, di far - ti pal - pi - tar,
di strin - ger ti al cuor mi - o, di far - ti pal - pi -

tar. Da te co - sì lon - ta - no io

sof - fro, io sof - fro as - sa - i; né pa - ce io tro - vo

ma - i per - chè trop - po è l'a - mor, [Ah!]

Ho! quant' io t'a - mo, o quan - to in me for - te è il de -

---

* At the bottom of the autograph manuscript Puccini wrote:

7

si - o, for - te è il de - si - o,

di strin-ger-ti al cuor mi - o, di far-ti pal-pi - tar,

di strin-ger-ti al cuor mi - o, di far - ti pal-pi - tar.

Da te co-sì lon - ta - no io sof-fro, io sof-fro as - sa - i;

rai___ tut - to ob - bli - ar. E dam-mi un ba - cio e il mon-do in -

tie - ro, e mi fa - rai tut-to ob - bli - ar.___ O mia vit -

to-ria, O mio te-sor sa - ra,___ O be - ne mio, O mi - o sol pen -

sie - ro, e dam-mi un ba - cio e il mon-do in - tie - ro, e mi fa -

rai tos - to ob - bli - ar! E dam - mi un ba - cio e il

mon - do in - tier, e mi fa - rai tos - to

ob - bli - ar! Ob - bli - ar!

Ob - bli - ar!_____

8va

* The above reading replaced:

rai_____ tos - to ob - bli -

12

1878 [?]   VEXILLA [REGIS PRODEUNT] A 2 VOCI

For Tenor and Bass Soli (or Two-part Men's Chorus) and Organ

Text by Venantius Honorius Clementianus Fortunatus (530–609)

THIS PASSIONTIDE PROCESSIONAL hymn reputedly dates from 19 November 569, when the fragmentary relics of the True Cross, sent by the Emperor Justin II to Queen Radegund, were received at the monastery in Poictiers. Since the tenth century, Fortunatus' text has assumed a traditional place as the vesper office hymn from Passion Sunday to the Wednesday in Holy Week. Puccini's setting of this hymn was commissioned by his Lucchese friend Adelson Betti for the little church in the fashionable mountain resort of Bagni di Lucca sometime between 1874 and 1880. Betti's son, Adolfo, described the circumstances of its origin in a letter written in English to William Oliver Strunk, a former chief of the Music Division at the Library of Congress:

> 27 April [1936]
> Hotel Ansonia
> Broadway at 73 Street
> New York City
>
> The piece is very simple and rather naive (it shows the master in his years of "apprentisage") but it is interesting as an example of his creative power in a field almost antagonistic to the one in which he achieved fame. It also has a rather amusing story. My father—Adelson Betti—an apothecary by profession, was an ardent lover of music and had many friends among the artists who used to visit our little village—Bagni di Lucca—then a famous summer resort.[1] [Giovanni] Sgambati, [Alfredo] Catalani, [Augusto] Rotoli, [Luigi] Denza, [Francesco Paolo] Tosti, Puccini (to name just a few) were frequent visitors in our home. Puccini, then a young student in Lucca (Istituto Musicale Pacini),[2] came often to Bagni to play at . . . [Betti's ellipses] the balls of the Casino (salary 10–15 lire per night—about one dollar). He usually arrived before the time of the show and took supper with us, occasionally showing to my father his latest compositions or playing excerpts from the operas he admired most. On one of these visits my father, who was acting organist and choirmaster of our little church, asked if he would write a ["little," crossed out] composition for one of the forthcoming festivities. Giacomo agreed. The price (!) was stipulated as follows: Ten lire cash (about 80 cents!) and . . . one of the special cakes for which Bagni di Lucca was famous! And so the "Vexilla" came into existence![3]

---

1. In 1909, Puccini composed part of Act II of *La fanciulla del West* at Bagni di Lucca. He spent the summers of 1919, 1920, and 1921 there and held some crucial secret meetings with Giuseppe Adami and Renato Simoni concerning the libretto of *Turandot*. The maid at the Hotel Queen Victoria remembers how Puccini told her not to disturb his papers in room 33 and how guests complained about Puccini's playing the piano in the *salottino* at all hours. (See B. Cherubini's article "A Bagni di Lucca nasce *Turandot*" in *La provincia di Lucca* [Lucca: Palazzo Provinciale, 1974].)

2. Now known as the Istituto Musicale Pareggiato "L. Boccherini."

3. Quoted in the *Report of the Librarian of Congress* (Washington, D.C.: 1935–1936), p. 40. Adolfo Betti (b. 21 March 1873, Bagni di Lucca; d. 2 December 1950) was an Italian violinist and the leader of the Flonzaley String Quartet. In 1920, Betti received the following note from Puccini dated 18 September: "So you go from country to country gathering praise and money. Bravo. I intend to return to Bagni di Lucca another year." Betti taught at the Brussels Conservatory and wrote *La vita e l'arte di Francesco Geminiani*, published in Lucca in 1933. That year, he was the recipient of the Coolidge medal for exceptional artistic merits.

The Library of Congress acquired the autograph manuscript from Adolfo Betti in 1936. The signed title page of this undated manuscript states: "Vexilla / a 2 Voci / G. Puccini." The text appears not to have been written in Puccini's hand. Previously unpublished, the present (and first) edition is faithful to Puccini's manuscript. The tenor part, originally written in the tenor clef, has been notated in the G clef; the organ part, originally written on two staves, has been distributed on three. Although Puccini only set the first two of the original eight stanzas of the hymn to music, the work is complete. It can be sung either by two solo voices or by a two-part chorus.

VEXILLA REGIS PRODEUNT

Vexilla Regis prodeunt, Vexilla Regis prodeunt:
Fulget Crucis, Fulget Crucis mysterium,
Qua vita mortem, mortem pertulit,
Et morte vitam, morte vitam protulit.
Vexilla Regis prodeunt: Fulget Crucis,
Crucis mysterium.

Quae vulnerata lanceae
Mucrone diro, diro, criminum,
Ut nos lavaret, lavaret sordibus,
Manavit unda, unda et sanguine.

Vexilla Regis prodeunt, Vexilla Regis prodeunt:
Fulget Crucis, Fulget Crucis mysterium,
Qua vita mortem, mortem pertulit,
Et morte vitam, morte vitam protulit.

Vexilla Regis prodeunt: Fulget Crucis,
Crucis mysterium.

THE STANDARDS OF THE KING GO FORTH

The standards of the King go forth:
Brightly gleams the mystery of the Cross,
By which life endured death
And by death gave back life.

[The Cross,] which wounded by the dread point of the lance,
Dripped water and blood.
And there issued forth water with blood
To cleanse us from sin.

The standards of the King go forth:
Brightly gleams the mystery of the Cross.

VEXILLA [REGIS PRODEUNT] A 2 VOCI

For Tenor and Bass Soli (or Two-part Men's Chorus) and Organ (or Harmonium)

First Edition

Text by
**VENANTIUS HONORIUS
CLEMENTIANUS FORTUNATUS**

Music by
GIACOMO PUCCINI
Edited by Michael Kaye

per - tu - lit, Et___ mor - te vi - tam,___ mor - te vi - tam

per - tu - lit, Et mor - te vi - tam,___ mor - te vi - tam

pro - tu - lit. Ve - xil - la Re - gis___ prod - e - unt:___

pro - tu - lit. Ve - xil - la Re - gis___ prod - e - unt:___

26

Ful - get Cru - cis, ___ Cru - cis my - ste - rium.*

Ful - get Cru - cis, ___ Cru - cis my - ste - ri - um.

Ped.

30 Largo

Largo

grave

Quae vul-ne-ra-ta lan - ceae† Mu - cro - ne ___

*

ste - ri - um.

† The MS states: "Que vulnerata lance."

19

di - ro,_____ di - ro,__ cri - mi - num, Quae vul - ne - ra - ta

lan - ceae Mu - cro - ne_____ di - ro, di - ro, cri - mi -

san-gui - ne.____ Ut nos la - va - ret, la - va - ret

san-gui - ne.____ Ut nos la - va - ret, la - va - ret

sor - di - bus, ma - na - vit un - da,____ un - da et san-gui - ne.____

sor - di - bus, ma - na - vit un - da,____ un - da et san-gui - ne.____

Ma - na - vit___ un - da___ ma - na - vit___ un - da et san ____ guine.*

Ma - na - vit, ma - na - vit un - da et san - gui - ne.

Maestoso

Ve - xil - la Re - gis_____ prod - e -

Ve - xil - la Re - gis_____ prod - e -

Maestoso

* san - gui - ne.

unt,_____ Ve - xil - la Re - gis_____ prod - e -

unt,_____ Ve - xil - la Re - gis_____ prod - e -

unt: Ful - get Cru - cis, Ful - get Cru - cis my -

unt: Cru - cis, Cru - cis my -

75

ste - rium,* Qua vi - ta mor - tem, mor - tem

ste - ri - um, Qua vi - ta mor - tem, mor - tem

79

per - tu - lit, Et___ mor - te vi - tam,___ mor - te vi - tam

per - tu - lit, Et mor - te vi - tam,___ mor - te vi - tam

*

ste - ri - um,

25

83

pro - tu-lit. Ve - xil - la Re - gis____ prod - e - unt:___

pro - tu-lit. Ve - xil - la Re - gis____ prod - e - unt:___

88

Ful - get Cru - cis,___ Cru - cis my - ste - rium.*

Ful - get Cru - cis,___ Cru - cis my - ste - ri - um.

Ped.

* ste - ri - um.

26

SALVE REGINA
For Soprano and Organ (Or Harmonium)
Text by Antonio Ghislanzoni

The text is not related to the office hymn that begins "Salve Regina."

THIS FERVENT SONG of praise in adoration of the Virgin Mary reputedly dates from the period 1878–1880, during Puccini's years as a church organist in Lucca. However, that assertion seems doubtful in view of the facts that he enrolled in the Milan Conservatory in 1880 and the first appearance of the text was not until 1882, when it was published as one of Ghislanzoni's *Melodie per Canto* in the second "augmented and corrected edition" of that collection of song texts published by Emilio Quadrio in Milan.[1] The manuscript of *Salve Regina* (two pages, 36 measures) is undated. Considering the bibliographical information pertaining to Ghislanzoni's text, the period 1882–1883 would seem to be a more appropriate time frame for this song. This is particularly so when one considers that in 1883 Puccini chose another one of Ghislanzoni's texts from the same volume of *Melodie per Canto*, "Noi leggevamo un giorno per diletto," for his song *Storiella d'amore*. Ghislanzoni's name does not appear on either the complete autograph or the single page of sketches for *Salve Regina*, but it is likely that at one time it was indicated on the complete autograph in the upper right corner, which has been torn off. Puccini also used *Salve Regina* in his first opera, *Le Villi* (begun in September of 1883 in Lucca and completed on 31 December of that year).[2] In *Le Villi*, *Salve Regina* (originally in F major) became the orchestral introduction to No. 5 (*Scena III^a*; in A major), and it formed the basis for the prayer "Angiol di Dio, che i vanni rivolgi al ciel stasera" (in E-flat major), sung first by the character Guglielmo (baritone). He is joined in the prayer by Anna (soprano),[3] then by Roberto (tenor), and, finally, by the entire chorus.

Antonio Ghislanzoni (b. 25 November 1824, Barco di Lecco; d. 16 July 1893, Caprino Bergamasco) was a prominent author and poet among Milan's exponents of *scapigliatura*, a literary movement in Italy dating from the 1860s. He is perhaps best remembered today as the librettist of Verdi's *Aida* (1871); actually, he translated the original French prose draft into Italian and versified the resulting libretto. The multitalented Ghislanzoni was also an ex-seminarist, a student of medicine, a contrabass player, and a well-known baritone. He made his operatic debut in Lodi in 1846 in *Luisa Strozzi* by Gualtiero Sanelli, and sang in Piacenza and at the Teatro Carcano during the 1847–1848 season. In 1849, he was

---

1. Ghislanzoni's *Salve Regina* was not, however, included in the first edition of *Melodie per Canto* published the previous year by Perussia e Quadrio Editori, Milan; nor was it part of an earlier collection entitled *Album di Romanze per Musica* (issued in Lecco in 1877 at Ghislanzoni's own expense as a bonus for subscribers to the *Giornale-Capriccio*, which he founded and directed).

2. The Italianized title *Le Villi* is used, for it is that title which is written in a very neat hand (possibly not Puccini's) on both the cover and the signed title page of a very interesting autograph manuscript of the "Opera in un Atto," dated (definitely in Puccini's hand) "[18]83 Lucca / 11bre 83 [and inserted on the line above that] e X^bre." This "Partitura" is comprised of fragmentary sketches, a piano-vocal score of the first version of the opera, as well as sections of the work in full score; it is part of the Mary Flagler Cary Music Collection on deposit in The Pierpont Morgan Library in New York City. On page 29, headed "Scena III^a Preghiera / Baritono Sopr: / Tenore e Coro," Puccini has written the title of the opera as "Le Willis"; however, it appears that he originally wrote the words "Le Villi" with an additional "V" superimposed on the initial "V" to form the "W." The final "s" was appended to the penultimate letter "i"—resulting in "Le Willis" (see footnote 3).

3. The *cartellone* of the première at the Teatro dal Verme, which announced the opera as "Le Willis," referred to the artist who created the role of Anna as "R[osina] Caponetti." Charles Jahant, one of the world's leading authorities on opera singers and the annals of operatic performance, informs me that she was better known as Caponetti-Bassi. In fact, on the title page of the manuscript of *Le Villi* (described in footnote 2) she is so named in Puccini's hand.

arrested by the French, deported to Corsica, and imprisoned; but in 1851 he sang the role of Carlo V in Verdi's *Ernani* at the Théâtre-Italien in Paris, having fled Italy the previous year for political reasons. He founded a small opera company that toured in France. His repertoire included the roles of Figaro in Rossini's *Il barbiere di Siviglia*, Dr. Malatesta in *Don Pasquale*, Belcore in *L'elisir d'amore*, Antonio and the Marquis in *Linda di Chamounix*, Enrico in *Lucia di Lammermoor*, and the title roles in *Rigoletto* and *Guglielmo Tell*. He appeared with many provincial Italian opera companies, was, for a short time, the impresario of the Teatro di Santa Radegonda, and sang at La Scala in 1859. As a raconteur, journalist, and critic, he claimed to have written some 2,162 articles. He directed Ricordi's *La Gazzetta Musicale* (1866) and founded several newspapers, including *Lo Straordinario* (1860), *Il Lombardo* (1861), *Figaro* (1864), *Rivista minima di scienze, lettere e arti* (1876), *Giornale-Capriccio* (1877), and the *Posta di Caprino*. Ghislanzoni's literary works include an amusing history of Milan from 1836 to 1848 (*Storia di Milano dal 1836 al 1848*, published posthumously in 1945), the successful *Gli artisti da teatro* (1856, first published in serial form in *Cosmorama Pittorico* [di Milano]), *Libro proibito, Libro serio*, and *Libro allegro* (1878–1882). Between 1886 and 1889, he compiled six volumes of humorous recollections, documents, and anecdotes entitled *Capricci letterari*.

In addition to his work on *Aida*, Ghislanzoni had previously collaborated with Verdi on the libretti of the Italian version of *Don Carlos* (1867) and the revision of *La forza del destino* (1869). In 1869, Ghislanzoni supplied Verdi with the second verse of the delightful song *Stornello*, first published in an album of six songs by Auber, Antonio Cagnoni (for whom Ghislanzoni wrote the libretto of *Papà Martin* in 1871), Mercadante, Federico Ricci, Ambroise Thomas, and Verdi. Ghislanzoni's *Reminiscenze artistiche* and *Libro serio* (1879) contain sections about Verdi and his residence at Sant'Agata. Ghislanzoni's other major libretti include *I promessi sposi*, based on the Manzoni novel, for Errico Petrella (1869); *Fosca* (1873) and *Salvator Rosa* (1874) for Antonio Carlos Gomes; the self-caricaturing *Il parlatore eterno* (composed 1873; published ca. 1898) and *I Lituani* (1874) for Amilcare Ponchielli, for whom he also supplied the text for a cantata honoring the memory of Gaetano Donizetti (first performed at the Teatro Riccardi in Bergamo, 13 September 1875; published in 1894); and *Edmea* (1886) for Alfredo Catalani. He also wrote scenarios for ballets and even worked as a choreographer.

In 1876, Puccini walked from Lucca to Pisa to see *Aida* at the Teatro Verdi, a significant event in the aspiring composer's life; many years later he came to know Ghislanzoni. While he was composing his second opera, *Edgar,* Puccini and his librettist, Ferdinando Fontana, were guests at Ghislanzoni's villa at Caprino Bergamasco, located on Lake Como. In his "intimate memoir of Giacomo Puccini," Dante del Fiorentino recounts an entertaining story about a party held at Ghislanzoni's to celebrate the appointment of one of Puccini's classmates to the faculty of the Liceo Benedetto Marcello. At one point during the party, Ghislanzoni played Romeo to Puccini's Juliet, while Mascagni accompanied the action on the piano.[4]

The present edition of *Salve Regina* is based on the manuscripts, which Puccini gave to the Istituto Musicale Luigi Boccherini in Lucca. Although "organ or harmonium" accompaniment is specified in the autograph sources, the piece may be successfully performed with piano accompaniment.

---

4. See Dante del Fiorentino, *Immortal Bohemian: An Intimate Memoir of Giacomo Puccini* (New York: Prentice-Hall, 1952), pp. 57–59.

GUGLIELMO. ANNA. ROBERTO.

UNA VERGINE. UNA DELLE VILLI. UNA CONTADINELLA.

Costume sketches from the first production of *Le Villi*.

SALVE REGINA	HAIL, QUEEN!
Salve, salve del ciel regina,	Hail, hail, Queen of heaven,
Madre degli infelici,	Mother of the unfortunate,
Stella del mar divin [*sic*],	Divine star of the sea,*
Stella del mar dall'immortal fulgor, salve.	Immortal bright star of the sea, Hail.
Tu accogli e benedici	You accept and bless
D'ogni sventura il pianto	The cry of every unfortunate creature.
D'un' sguardo Tuo fai santo	With a glance, you sanctify
Ogni terreno amor,	Every earthly love.
D'uno sguardo Tuo fai santo	With just one glance, you sanctify
Ogni terreno amor.	Every earthly love.

The second strophe of Ghislanzoni's poem, which Puccini did not set to music, reads: "Te, nella veglia bruna, / Noma il fanciul gemendo, / Te, nella rea fortuna, / Invoca il pio nocchier. / Tu sull'abbisso orrendo / Il disperato arresti, / E di splendor celesti / Irradii il suo pensier."

---

*In English this translation is considered heretical. A theologically more acceptable translation of this line is "Blessed Mother of the sea," an allusion to another office hymn, *Ave Maris Stella*.

SALVE REGINA

For Soprano and Organ (or Harmonium)

Text by
ANTONIO GHISLANZONI

Music by
GIACOMO PUCCINI
Edited by Michael Kaye

Sal - ve; sal - ve del ciel, del ciel re -

---

* The autograph sketch is marked "Andante religioso."

"MENTÌA L'AVVISO"

Recitative and Aria for Tenor and Piano
Text by Felice Romani

The text is from Romani's melodrama *La solitaria delle Asturie, ossia La Spagna ricuperata.*

PUCCINI WROTE THIS dramatic scene and aria in June 1883 in fulfillment of the requirements for graduation from the Milan Conservatory (Conservatorio di Musica Giuseppe Verdi). The piece exists in two versions, the manuscripts of which are both preserved at the conservatory.

The signed cover of MS I identifies the work as an "Elaborato / dell'alunno Sig. Puccini," followed by the indication "I (pg. 3–7)." It consists of five pages of music (115 measures); at the bottom of the first page of music is the nonautograph indication "Ricevuto alle ore 6½ pom [-eridiane]." On the last page (originally numbered "7," but now numbered "5"),[1] are the signatures of "G. Puccini" and those of his teachers "A[ntonio] Bazzini / A[milcare] Ponchielli" and judges "A. Panzini / [Michele] Saladino / [Cesare] Dominiceti."

The first page of MS II states: "II (pg. 1–5) I° esame (Ideale) ore 6 pomeridiane / domenica 10 giugno 1883," with "Parole di Felice Romani" (the only reference to the text) written above the music in Puccini's hand. It appears to be a draft, as it contains several crossed out measures, shorthand notations (e.g., "2ª volta col canto sempre"), alterations, and variants from the version signed by the faculty. Some of its sections are written out of order but the entire work is sketched out on five pages. On the last page, after the music and three heavily crossed out lines, is Puccini's autograph apology: "Pietà un dolor di denti noioso che mi ha tormentato dalle 7 alle 2" ("Have mercy! a wearisome toothache that has been bothering me from 7 to 2 has started again"). In both manuscripts, the voice part is notated in the tenor clef; each includes the indication "Ten[ore] e P[iano] f[orte]."

The Milan Conservatory also owns a lithographed score for voice and piano in a copyist's hand based on MS I. (It was possibly intended for publication but it lacks a title page or any publication data.) This score may have been prepared as a scholastic exercise by another student in the conservatory's composition program, or it may have been prepared for Puccini so that he would have a neat presentation copy to show potential publishers.[2] All of these sources have been consulted in the preparation of the present edition; variants in manuscripts I and II are indicated throughout the music.

The word "Ideale" written in parentheses at the top of MS II of the "elaborato" has been misinterpreted as a title by many who have written about Puccini, leading one to believe that he wrote a song by that title when in fact he did not. The term "ideale" was used to describe a type of free-form composition.

In a letter to his father dated 12 October 1882, Pietro Mascagni, Puccini's onetime roommate and fellow student, described the entrance examinations for the Milan Conservatory:

---

1. A facsimile of page "7" is printed facing page 62 of Cecil Hopkinson's *Bibliography of the Works of Giacomo Puccini.* The pagination of the manuscript has evidently been altered since the publication of Hopkinson's bibliography.

2. Puccini's often difficult to decipher handwriting was a major reason for the failure of his opera *Le Villi* to rate even an honorable mention in the Sonzogno competition for one-act operas. Puccini referred to it as his "cacografia." According to Puccini's friend and biographer Arnaldo Fraccaroli (writing in *La Lettura*), one of the copyists employed by the Casa Ricordi threw up his arms for joy at having succeeded in deciphering a page of Puccini's manuscript. To these copyists, the announcement of a new Puccini opera was reason to worry.

I have finally stopped worrying all the time about the exams. . . . When I went to the Conservatory I was as white as a sheet and I stayed all by myself in a corner with my music under my arm. . . . Then, with a sure stride, I entered the room where the Commission was seated. It included Bazzini, Ponchielli, Domenicati [sic], Galli, Panzini and one other. . . . Those six professors, the best in Italy, were holding and poring over my music as a representative sent by the state would. . . . I take the note that had been handed to me and read: "Imitations" . . . a bass on which, at the piano, I have to improvise a harmonization. "If you want to practice a bit you may do so," Bazzini says to me. "Go ahead," I am told by the members of the Commission, "the second and the third in F." To make it short, I couldn't find the right chord after the F. I realized that I had lost my nerve and I got up, saying that I didn't think I could go on. The members of the Commission declared themselves satisfied and let me go after returning my music. I learned afterward that they had forgotten to give me the "ideale" exam and I was very sorry about that because I know that in that field I would have excelled. But Ponchielli seemed satisfied with what I had done and said he was sure I would be accepted.[3]

Puccini graduated from the Milan Conservatory with high honors ("Diploma superiore con medaglia di rame") on 16 July 1883:

Avendo il signor Puccini Giacomo di Lucca,
allievo di Composizione in codesto Istituto
in seguito agli esami di Licenza superato di
163/200 il numero dei punti di merito richiesti
per ottenere il Diploma onde si onorano gli alunni
distinti, gli viene rilasciato il presente,
munito del suggello del Conservatorio[4]

La Musica Popolare of 26 July proclaimed: "What was admired most in Puccini, more than the student who had completed his studies, was an assured musician with his own individuality who, inspired by his own imagination, writes without showing allegiance to any fashionable idol. . . . [Armando] Seppili and Puccini, here are two young men for whom everything points to a wonderful career."

The text by Felice Romani[5] is from his melodrama entitled *La solitaria delle Asturie, ossia La Spagna ricuperata,* first set to music by Carlo Coccia (La Scala, Milan, 6 March 1838) and subsequently set by Saverio Mercadante (Teatro la Fenice, Venice, 12 March 1840); Vincenzo Mela (1840); Luigi Ricci (Imperiale Teatro d'Odessa, Russia, 20 February 1845); and Giuseppe

---

3. Quoted in Edoardo Pompei, *Pietro Mascagni nella vita e nell'arte* (Rome: Tipografia Editrice Nazionale, 1912), pp. 26–29.

4. "[Be it known that] Mr. Giacomo Puccini of Lucca, student of Composition in this school, having received in the final exams 163 out of 200, more than the required number needed to obtain the certificate with which distinguished students are honored, the present diploma, imprinted with the seal of this Conservatory, is issued to him."

5. Felice Romani (b. 31 January 1788, Genoa; d. 28 January 1865, Moneglia) was one of the most important Italian librettists of the nineteenth century. He abandoned a career in law to write for the lyric stage and he supplied numerous composers with well over one hundred libretti (some of which were set to music by several different composers). Among his most important libretti are *La rosa bianca* and *Medea in Corinto* for Johann Simon Mayr (both in 1813); *Il Turco in Italia* for Rossini (1814); *Margherita d'Anjou* for Meyerbeer (1820); *Anna Bolena* (1830), *L'elisir d'amore* (1832), et al., for Donizetti; *Il Pirata* (1827), *La Straniera* (1829), *Zaira* (1829), *I Capuleti ed i Montecchi* (1830), *La Sonnambula* (1831), *Norma* (1831), and *Beatrice di Tenda* (1833), all for Bellini; and *Un giorno di regno* for Verdi (1840).

Sordelli, Jr. (Teatro Nobile, Pavia, 1846). In Romani's words, the plot concerns "Florinda, the daughter of Count Giuliano, disgraced by King Rodrigo, who provoked her father's vengeance against the king. Her father called for the Moors to come from Africa to Spain, and caused the massacre of the Goths: it is also well known that Florinda was so hated by the Spaniards that they named her *Cava*, which means *evil*. Florinda, tormented by remorse, could not survive her own shame," and so on.[6] The notes Puccini kept for one of his required studies in poetic and dramatic literature, taught at the Milan Conservatory in 1882–1883 by Prof. Ludovico Corio, preserve young Giacomo's reaction to such dramaturgy: "Ohimè!!!! Ahì! O Dio!!! Ajuto per carità!!! Basta!!! È troppo!!!"; "Ciao, professore...io dormo"; "Muojo!!!"[7]

According to the libretto of *La solitaria*, Gusmano was a "Condottiere dell'esercito Moro, che poi si scopre pel Conte Giuliano" ("Captain in the Moorish army, who is later discoverd to be Count Giuliano"). The excerpt set by Puccini occurs in the second scene of Act IV, the *mise en scène* of which is described in the libretto as: "a large cave in the valley of Ausena which penetrates deeply into the mountain through several subterranean passageways. Upstage there is an opening through which the sky is visible. It is evening. Several squadrons of Moors enter with lighted torches. They are led by Gusmano and Manuza, another captain of the Moors." After they sing a brief chorus, Manuza and the squadrons exit, leaving Gusmano alone on stage for the recitative and aria that begins "Mentìa l'avviso." Puccini did not set Romani's final quatrain, which reads: "In these shadows of the dark and blind night, Oh God of my fathers whom I have lost, unseen, I kneel, and ask your mercy." He used the second Lento theme as the basis for the famous tenor aria "Donna non vidi mai," sung by Renato des Grieux in Act I of *Manon Lescaut* (1893); the same theme is played by the orchestra earlier in the act to symbolize des Grieux's fascination with Manon. The piano part is appropriately operatic, more closely resembling a piano reduction of an orchestral accompaniment than music conceived for the keyboard, but there is no evidence to date that an orchestration was ever made or that the work was ever published in Puccini's lifetime. The first line of the sung text in the autographs is definitely "Mentìa l'avviso" and not "Menti all'avviso," as is often found in writings on Puccini and heard on recordings of the music made by internationally known sopranos.

---

6. The quotations from Romani's libretto are taken from the text as set to music by Mercadante.
7. Puccini's student notebooks are preserved at the Istituto Musicale Pareggiato "L. Boccherini" in Lucca.

MENTÌA L'AVVISO

[*Gusmano, solo, ritorna indietro pensoso. Annotta a poco a poco.*]
[Gusmano:]
Mentìa l'avviso . . . Eppur d'Ausena è questa
L'angusta valle . . . e qui fatal dimora
Mi presagiva la segreta voce
Che turba da più notti il mio riposo, il mio riposo.
Tu cui nomar non oso,
Tu! funesta donna, dall'avel risorta
Per mio supplizio, un'altra volta ancora
Promettesti vedermi . . . e in rio momento.
   Ah! chi geme? . . . M'inganno . . . è l'onda, è il vento.
     È la notte che mi reca
     Le sue larve, i suoi timori,
     Che gli accenti punitori
     Del rimorso udir mi fa.

THE WARNING WAS FALSE

[*Lost in thought, Gusmano, alone, reenters upstage. Night falls gradually.*]
[Gusmano:]
The warning was false . . . And yet, this is the narrow
Valley of Ausena . . . and here the fatal abode,
The place that the secret voice portended,
A voice that for many nights disturbed my rest.
You, whom I dare not name,
You, woeful woman, resurrected from the tomb
At my entreaty, you swore
You would see me once again . . . in an evil moment.
   Ah! Who is moaning? . . . I am mistaken . . . it is just the sound
     of a wave, it is the wind.
      It is the night which brings me
      Its ghosts, its fears,
      And makes me hear accusing words
      Of remorse.

MENTÌA L'AVVISO

Recitative and Aria for Tenor and Piano

Text by
FELICE ROMANI
(from the melodrama
La solitaria delle Asturie,
ossia La Spagna ricuperata)

Music by
GIACOMO PUCCINI
Edited by Michael Kaye

* The indications in pointed brackets appear in MS II.

e qui fa - tal di - mo - ra Mi pre - sa -
gi - va la se - gre - ta vo - ce Che tur - ba da più not

MS II:

molto rall.

rit.

ti il mio ri - po - so, il mio ri - po - so.

molto rall.

rit.

* MS II:

po - so.

Allegro

sf ⟨pp⟩

39

vol - ta an - co - ra   Pro - met - te - sti ve - der - mi... e in rio mo - men - to.

Ah!   chi ge - me?... M'in - gan - no...

MS II:

dolce [a tempo]

Lento

è l'on-da, è il ven - to. È la not - te che__ mi re - ca Le sue lar - ve, i suoi ti - mo - ri, Che gli ac - cen - ti pu - ni - to - ri__ Del ri - mor - so u - dir mi fa. È la not - - -

Lento

te   Che il ri - mor - so u - dir mi

fa._____

[a tempo]

È   la not - te   che___ mi re - ca   Le sue

lar - ve,   i suoi ti - mo - ri,   È   la not - te   che mi

re - ca Le sue lar - ve e i suoi ti - mor.___ È la

not - te che il ri - mor - so u - dir mi fa, u - dir mi

fa.

STORIELLA D'AMORE, Melodia[1]

Text by Antonio Ghislanzoni

OF THE POEMS by Ghislanzoni that Puccini chose to set to music, the one entitled "Noi leggevamo un giorno per diletto" became Puccini's first published composition. The music was completed before 4 October 1883, for it appeared in the musical appendix to Edoardo Sonzogno's weekly illustrated periodical *La Musica Popolare*, which proudly announced:

> Today's issue of *Musica Popolare* contains a work by the young maestro Giacomo Puccini, one of the most distinguished students to graduate this year from the Milan Conservatory, who is already favorably known in the world of music for one of his noteworthy instrumental works performed with great success at the close of this past academic year at our best institute of music. . . . Giovanni [*sic*] Puccini studied music first with Angeloni in Puccini's native city, and then with Bazzini and Ponchielli in Milan; he has written a Mass for four-part chorus and orchestra, which was greeted with approbation at the Lucca Cathedral, and different smaller chamber compositions. Art can expect much from his talent.[2]

The article, headed "La Nostra Musica," also mentioned the five generations of the musical Puccini family, and concluded with the comment that when one says the word "composer" in Lucca it is synonymous with "Puccini." Earlier that year (on 1 April), Sonzogno's other periodical, *Il Teatro Illustrato*, announced its first competition for young unknown Italian composers to write a one-act opera (prize: two thousand lire). Entries had to be submitted by 31 December 1883 in order to be eligible. During his final months as a student at the Milan Conservatory, Puccini decided to enter the Sonzogno competition, but his final examinations (24 June) and graduation (16 July) delayed the search for a libretto. The completion of his graduation composition referred to in *La Musica Popolare*—a *Capriccio sinfonico* for orchestra—received priority attention.[3] Upon completion of his graduation, Puccini was free to begin the search for a libretto for his first opera. Amilcare Ponchielli was responsible for introducing Puccini to Ferdinando Fontana and for initiating their collaboration on *Le Villi*, composed during the summer and fall of 1883 and submitted to the Sonzogno competition at the last possible moment (on 31 December).

Puccini was well known to the judges of the competition (they were Ponchielli, Cesare Dominiceti, Franco Faccio and Amintore Galli).[4] *Storiella d'amore* had appeared in a Sonzogno publication only three months before the deadline for the contest. Given these circumstances, it is rather surprising that Puccini was not even awarded an honorable mention when the contest results were announced. However, Amintore Galli, Puccini's professor for the history and

---

1. Certain of Puccini's biographers have misquoted the title as "Noi legger" or "Noi leggeramo." Others have mistakenly attributed the text to Puccini himself. "Storiella d'amore / (Melodia)" is the title that appears on the first published edition of 1883. Ghislanzoni's name was omitted from that publication, but it appears in Puccini's hand above the title in the upper right corner of the autograph sketch for the song "Noi leggevamo insieme / parole di A. Ghislanzoni." See p. 27.

2. *La Musica Popolare*, Anno II, No. 40, 4 October 1883.

3. Rehearsals began on 10 July for the première of the *Capriccio sinfonico*, performed on 14 July by a largely student orchestra led by a guest conductor, the composer Franco Faccio (1840–1891). Additional performances were given on 15 and 16 July. The following year (on 6 July 1884), Faccio included the work in a concert held in celebration of the Italian General Exposition.

4. According to *Il Teatro Illustrato* of April 1884 (Anno IV, No. 40, p. 50), a fifth judge, the composer Pietro Platania (1828–1907), had to withdraw from adjudicating in order to return to Palermo.

aesthetics of music at the Milan Conservatory and the director of music publications for Sonzogno, wrote the following review of the première of *Le Villi* in *Il Secolo*:

> Saturday and Sunday evening we attended the first two performances of the opera-ballo *Le Villi* given at the Dal Verme; music by maestro *Puccini*, the very distinguished student of our conservatory. The opera was a total success, warmly received by the audience, which was at times very enthusiastic. Not a single sung number passed by in silence; and as for the instrumental music which closes the first part, it was played no less than *three* times at the première as well as at the second performance. They called for the composer after the *Chorus* and its successive *Waltzer*, as they did again after the *Duet* and grandiose *Prayer*, and again after the *Ritornello* in the instrumental piece: a brief stroke but it succeeded marvelously.[5]

When thirteen performances of the revised two-act version of *Le Villi* were given at La Scala in 1885, the conductor was none other than Franco Faccio.[6] As fate would have it, Puccini became a protégé of the publisher Giulio Ricordi and one of the Casa Ricordi's most profitable composers in the history of that famous firm. The Casa Musicale Sonzogno would not play a role in the story of Puccini's published works until the composition of *La Rondine*.

The musical form of *Storiella d'amore* is that of a simple strophic song. In it, Puccini already manifests numerous characteristics of his distinctive melodic style and harmonic language. In the accompaniment, he employs a device that would serve him well throughout his career. This particular device involves a series of repeated chords or notes played either on the offbeat, or syncopated.[7] In *Storiella d'amore*, chords are played on the offbeat by the right hand, underlining the main theme, while the left hand doubles the vocal line. Also characteristic of Puccini is the abundance of performance instructions regarding expression, phrasing, tempo, and dynamics; e.g., "con anima stent[ato] rit[ardando] piano a tempo affrett[ando] piano," all within the space of nine beats of the basic tempo marked "Andantino mosso" (see measures 28–30). The Lento theme of *Storiella d'amore* (measures 44–48) was to provide Puccini with material for the trio for soprano, tenor, and baritone in Act III of *Edgar* (1889): first thematically, at Edgar's line "Io vi chieggo pietà per quei ginocchi"; then exactly, at Tigrana's words "Silenzio, frate, lasciatemi pregar!"; then again, beginning with Edgar's "Un detto della tua bocca vermiglia" and Tigrana's "V'allontanate! Lasciatemi pregar!" (see musical example).[8]

5. *Il Secolo* was also owned by Edoardo Sonzogno. Galli's review was reprinted in *La Lettura* of 1 April 1923 (Anno XXIII, No. 4, p. 304). *Il Teatro Illustrato* of June 1884 published a very favorable review of the première as well.

6. See *La Scala, 1778–1906 note storiche e statistiche*, 5th ed. (Milan: G. Ricordi, 1907).

7. In Puccini's orchestrated accompaniments these syncopations are played by various combinations of instruments (oboes and violas; four horns; oboes [English horn], clarinets, and bassoons; strings *in divisi*) while some of the first violins and/or a solo instrument double the melody, depending on the desired effect.

8. Puccini retained this trio in all subsequent revisions of *Edgar*.

There is also a similarity between the following section of Mimì's aria sung in Act I of *La Bohème* (1896):

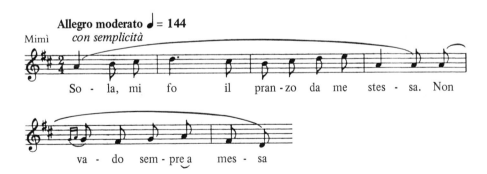

47

and this phrase from *Storiella d'amore* (both are marked *con semplicità* and both are in D major), written some thirteen years earlier:

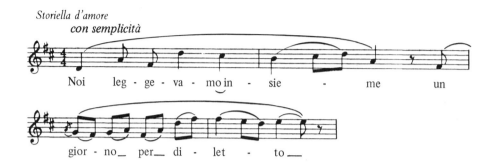

The present edition is based on the autograph sketches preserved along with other Puccini manuscripts at the Istituto Musicale Pareggiato "L. Boccherini" in Lucca,[9] and the Sonzogno edition of 1883.

Antonio Ghislanzoni's poem is a version of an account of the illicit love between Paolo, the son of Malatesta da Verrucchio, and Francesca da Rimini, the daughter of Guido Minore da Polenta, a powerful citizen of Ravenna. These actual lovers were immortalized by Dante Alighieri in the *Divine Comedy*. In Canto V of the *Inferno*, Francesca relates to Dante how she and Paolo had fallen in love while reading together from the French prose romance of *Lancelot of the Lake*:

> Noi leggiavamo un giorno per diletto
> Di Lancialotto, come amor lo strinse;
> Soli eravamo e senza alcun sospetto;

Ghislanzoni's amusing poem might be interpreted as Paolo's retelling of the story.[10]

In measure numbers 54–56, the editor suggests:

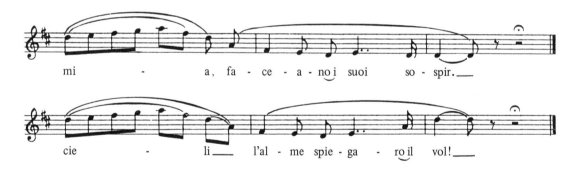

---

9. A facsimile of one of these sketches is published in Giorgio Magri's *Puccini e le sue rime,* p. 40.

10. The legend of the tragic romance of Paolo and Francesca, one of the most famous in Western literature, is based on actual events that occurred in the late thirteenth century. Dante's account of their passion has been a favorite theme for artists, authors, and composers (including Liszt, Rossini, Thomas, Tchaikovsky, Rachmaninov, and Zandonai). Six years after the publication of Puccini's *Storiella d'amore*, Amilcare Ponchielli wrote a song for voice and piano on this same Ghislanzoni text; it remains among his unpublished compositions.

STORIELLA D'AMORE (Melodia)

Noi leggevamo insieme un giorno per diletto
Una gentile istoria piena di mesti amor;
E senz'alcun sospetto ella sedeami a lato,
Sul libro avventurato intenta il guardo e il cor.

Noi leggevamo insieme, Ah! Ah!

L'onda de' suoi capelli il volto a me lambia,
Eco alla voce mia,
Eco faceano i suoi sospir.

Gli occhi dal libro alzando
Nel suo celeste viso,
Io vidi in un sorriso
Riflesso il mio desir.

La bella mano al core strinsi di gioia ansante . . .
Nè più leggemmo avante . . .
E cadde il libro al suol.

Noi leggevamo insieme, Ah! Ah!

Un lungo, ardente bacio congiunse i labbri aneli,
E ad ignorati cieli
L'alme spiegaro il vol.

LITTLE STORY OF LOVE (Melody)

One day, we were reading together for pleasure
A pleasant story fraught with sad love;
She sat beside me without any misgiving,
Her gaze and her heart intent upon the fateful book.

We were reading together, Ah! Ah!

Her wavy hair caressed my face,
Her sighs were echoing my voice,
Echoing my voice.

Raising my eyes from the book,
I saw my desire reflected in a smile
Upon her heavenly face.

Panting with joy, I pressed her lovely hand to my heart . . .
We read no further . . .
And the book fell to the ground.

We were reading together, Ah! Ah!

A long, ardent kiss united our yearning lips,
And toward unknown skies
Our souls unfolded in flight.

STORIELLA D'AMORE, Melodia

"Noi leggevamo insieme"

Text by
ANTONIO GHISLANZONI

Music by
GIACOMO PUCCINI

Edited by Michael Kaye

Noi leg-ge-va-mo in-sie - me un gior-no_per-di - let - to__
Gli oc-chi dal li-bro al - zan - do Nel suo_ce-le-ste_vi - so,__

U - na gen-ti-le i - sto - ria___ pie - na di me-sti a - mor.___
Io vi-di in un sor - ri - so___ Ri - fles-so il mio de - sir,___

allarg.

U - na gen-ti-le i - sto - ri - a pie - na di me - sti a-mor;___ E
Io vi-di in un sor - ri - so Ri - fles-so il mio de - sir.___ La

allarg.

sen - z'al - cun so - spet - to el - la se - de -
bel - la ma - no al co - re strin - si di gio -

51

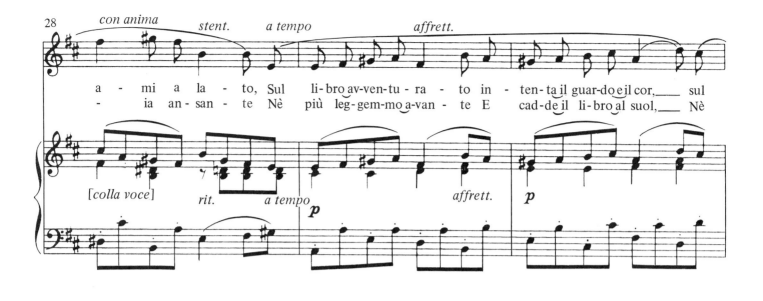

a - mi a la - to, Sul li - bro av-ven-tu - ra - to in - ten-ta il guar-do e il cor,___ sul
- ia an-san - te Nè più leg-gem-mo a-van - te E cad-de il li-bro al suol,___ Nè

li - bro av-ven-tu - ra - to in - ten-ta il guar-do e il cor.___ Noi leg-ge-
più leg-gem-mo a-van - te E cad-de il li-bro al suol.___ Noi leg-ge-

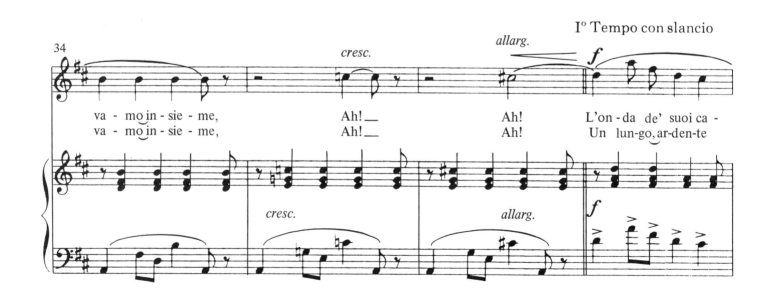

va - mo in - sie - me, Ah!___ Ah! L'on - da de' suoi ca -
va - mo in - sie - me, Ah!___ Ah! Un lun-go, ar-den-te

pel - li il vol - to a me _ lam - bi - a, _ il vol-to a me lam-
ba - cio con - giun - se i lab - bri a - ne - li, _ con - giun-se i lab - bri a -

bi - a,
ne - li,

E-co al-la vo - ce _ mi -
E ad i-gno - ra - ti _ cie -

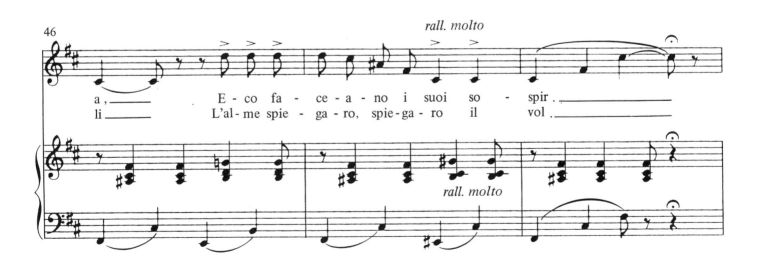

a, _ E - co fa - ce-a-no i suoi so - spir. _
li _ L'al - me spie - ga-ro, spie-ga-ro il vol. _

53

L'on - da dei suoi ca - pel - li ___ il vol - to a me lam - bi - a,
Un lun - go, ar - den - te ba - cio ___ con - giun - se i lab - bri a - ne - li,

E - co al - la vo - ce ___ mi - a, fa - ce - a - no i suoi so -
E ad i - gno - ra - ti ___ cie - li L'al - me spie - ga - ro il

spir. ___
vol. ___

[D. S.]

[Per finire]
Fine

SOLE E AMORE, Mattinata

Text by an anonymous author (probably Puccini)

THIS BEAUTIFUL SALON SONG first appeared in the musical supplement to the magazine entitled *Paganini*, a "Periodico Artistico-Musicale" published in Genoa in 1888 (Anno II, No. 23).[1] The previous year, Giuseppe Verdi, who was then in Genoa for rehearsals of *Otello*, had encouraged his friend Camillo Sivori to publish *Paganini*. Sivori (b. 25 October 1815, Genoa; d. there, 19 February 1894) was a famous Italian violinist who had studied with Niccolò Paganinï and modeled his style of violin playing after that of the legendary virtuoso. He also composed numerous pieces for the violin. Sivori's *Paganini* was issued for five seasons, from 1887 to 1892. In addition to Puccini, composers who had works published in *Paganini* included Alfredo Catalani, Alberto Franchetti, Luigi Mancinelli, Niccolò Massa, Alessandro Longo, Giovanni Tebaldini, Marco Sala, Sivori, and others.[2]

Puccini's autograph manuscript of a preliminary draft of *Sole e amore* reveals that "il 1° di marzo dell'ottanotto" was originally the last line of the sung text:[3]

il pri - mo_ di_ mar - zo dell' ot - tan - ot - to __

and it probably signifies the date of composition (1 March 1888).[4] The change of this line to the dedication "Al *Paganini*, G. Puccini" in the published version is in keeping with Puccini's sense of humor and penchant for practical jokes.

The autograph draft version is untitled, and neither it nor a copyist's proof of the *Paganini* edition attributes the text to anyone.[5] Parts of the text may be an adaptation or a parody of a well-known sonnet entitled "Mattinata," No. LII of the *Rime Nuove* by Giosue Carducci, which begins:

> Batte a la tua finestra, e dice, il sole:
> —Levati, bella, ch'è tempo d'amare.

In Carducci's "Mattinata" one also finds the lines:

> Batte al tuo cor, ch'è un bel giardino in fiore,
> Il mio pensiero, e dice: —Si può entrare?

---

1. This issue of *Paganini* was designated as a "Numero Strenno." (It also included Catalani's *A Sera*, a work for solo piano that was subsequently arranged for string quartet ca. 1889-1890. *A Sera* was ultimately used for the prelude to Act III of Catalani's *La Wally*, first performed at La Scala on 20 January 1892.)

2. See Giuliano Balestrieri's article entitled "Musetta è nata in barca" (*La Scala*, No. 15, 15 January 1951, p. 34), which includes a photograph of the cover of the issue of *Paganini* containing *Sole e amore*.

3. Facsimiles of this manuscript are reproduced in Antonio Conti's article "Un inedito di Verdi / Un inedito di Puccini" in *La Lettura* (Anno XXXIX, No. 9, September 1939), pp. 807–13, and in *Rassegna Musicale* (Milan: Curci, March 1969), p. 24.

4. Ernesto Paolone suggests that if "il 1° di marzo dell'ottanotto" was not the date of composition, it might have been noted in tender recollection of some amorous adventure (see *Rassegna Musicale*, pp. 23–25).

5. The proof, which is owned by the Milan Conservatory, contains numerous errors in both the voice and piano parts. These errors were corrected in the *Paganini* edition.

Carducci (b. 27 July 1835, Val di Castello; d. 16 February 1907, Bologna) was one of Italy's most beloved and prolific poets.[6]

Puccini obviously remembered *Sole e amore* when he was writing *La Bohème*. It is used in that opera to conclude the third act, where it forms the basis of the famous quartet (more appropriately described as a double duet for Mimì and Rodolfo and Musetta and Marcello), which begins "Addio dolce svegliare alla mattina" and which is also in G-flat major. Ten years after the première of *La Bohème*, Puccini acknowledged this act of self-borrowing by inscribing the autograph draft of *Sole e amore* to his friend, the composer Francesco Paolo Tosti:[7]

al mio carissimo F. P. Tosti
questo germe primo
di *Bohème*
Milano G. Puccini
1. aprile [1]906

("To my dearest friend F. P. Tosti this first embryo of *Bohème*.")

Puccini probably dedicated this manuscript of *Sole e amore* to Tosti in anticipation of the older composer's sixtieth birthday.[8]

At one point while he was composing *Sole e amore*, Puccini apparently considered a different setting for the voice at measures 24–27. At that position the autograph draft differs from the *Paganini* edition and reads as follows:

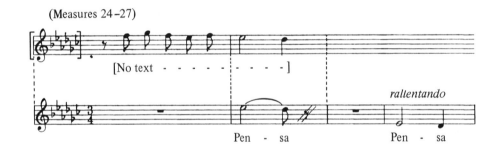

(Measures 24–27)

Based on the aforementioned sources, the present edition retains the somewhat unconventional but expressive phrasing marks found in Puccini's manuscript.

---

6. Carducci was also a publisher, an author and educator, and a professor of literature at the University of Bologna from 1860 to 1903. The collected edition of his poetry spans the period from 1850 to 1900 and the *Rime Nuove* date from 1861 to 1887. Honored as an Italian senator in 1906, Carducci is considered the national poet of modern Italy.

7. Tosti (b. 9 April 1846, Ortona, Abruzzi; d. 2 December 1916, Rome) is best remembered for his songs for voice and piano. Tosti achieved great popularity in England, where in 1880 he served the royal family as music master and in 1894 he taught at the Royal Academy of Music. He was knighted in 1908. It was in Tosti's London home about 1904 that Puccini first met Sybil Seligman, who for twenty years shared an intimate and complex relationship with Puccini as a lover, confidante, mentor, and friend.

8. On 15 April 1906, Puccini, Tosti, and their wives dined at the Albergo Ristorante della Ferrata in Milan in the company of friends (including Giulio Ricordi, Ernesto Consolo, Marco Praga, and Gabriele D'Annunzio) for a belated celebration of Tosti's birthday.

SOLE E AMORE, Mattinata

Il sole allegramente batte ai tuoi vetri;
Amor pian pian batte al tuo cuore
E l'uno e l'altro chiama.
Il sole dice: "O dormente mostrati che sei bella!"
Dice l'amor: "Sorella, col tuo primo pensier
Pensa a chi t'ama! Pensa a chi t'ama!
Pensa!"

Al Paganini, G. Puccini

SUN AND LOVE, Morning Song

The sun joyfully taps at your windows;
Love very softly taps at your heart,
And they are both calling you.
The sun says: "Oh sleeper, show yourself for you are beautiful!"
Love says: "Sister, with your first thought
Think of the one who loves you! Think of who loves you!
Think!"

To Paganini, G. Puccini

SOLE E AMORE
(Mattinata)

Text by an anonymous
author (probably Puccini)

Music by
GIACOMO PUCCINI

Edited by Michael Kaye

* The indications in parentheses appear only in the *Paganini* edition.

58

bel - la!" Di-ce l'a-mor: "So - rel - la, col tuo pri-mo pen - sier

Pen - sa a chi t'a - ma! Pen-sa a chi t'a - ma!

Pen - sa!" Al Pa - ga -

ni - ni, G. Puc-ci - ni

_____

* The *Paganini* edition states merely "con espress."

Photograph dating from the time that Puccini composed *Avanti Urania!*

AVANTI *URANIA!*
Text by Renato Fucini

IN THE LITERATURE pertaining to Puccini's life and works, the most prevalent, but inaccurate, descriptions of this song are "a marching song," "for chorus and piano," "composed for the launching of a ship," "dating from 1899 [*sic*]."[1] The nautical vessel in question has often been referred to as a "yacht" owned by Marchese Carlo Ginori-Lisci.

On 18 December 1895, Puccini wrote the following letter to Ginori-Lisci:

Milano Via Solferino 27

Uno speciale ringraziamento per tutte le gentilezze che Ella ha voluto sempre usarmi . . . ultima quella del regolare permesso per il capanno, cosa della quale ne restai oltremodo contento.

Fui dolentissimo non poterla salutare lunedì sera come speravo ma la politica me lo rapì! *L'Avanti Urania* sarà pronto al più presto possibile . . . fin adesso non potei causa il gran da fare che me ha dato l'ultimo atto di *Bohème* che io desiderei tanto fosse a Lei dedicata: Accetta? Gliene sarebbe gratissimo il suo aff amico

Giacomo Puccini

A special thank you for all the kindnesses you have always shown me . . . the latest one [being] the permit for the shooting box [at Torre del Lago] which really pleased me.

I was very sorry not to have been able to say goodbye to you on Monday night, but politics precluded my doing so! *Avanti Urania* will be ready as soon as possible . . . I haven't been able to get to it until now because of the enormous work I had to do on the last act of *Bohème* which I would like very much to dedicate to you. Do you accept? Your affectionate friend Giacomo Puccini would be very grateful to you.[2]

In this letter, Puccini was referring to the spirited song for voice and piano entitled *Avanti Urania!*, which he completed at Torre del Lago on 4 October 1896 to celebrate Marchese Ginori-Lisci's acquisition of the Scottish-built 179-ton iron screw steamer, the ex-*Queen Mary*, and its subsequent launching under the Italian flag as the *Urania*.[3] Marchese Carlo Benedetto Ginori-Lisci (b. 1851, Florence; d. 1905, Munich) was a wealthy Italian industrialist, patron of the arts, and a direct descendant of Carlo Lorenzo Ginori (1702–1757), the famous porcelain and ceramics artist whose works rank among some of the finest in Europe. (In the early part of the eighteenth century, Marchese

---

1. In his book *Puccini e le sue rime* (p. 317) and in his article "Una ricetta di Puccini" (in *Critica pucciniana* [Lucca, 1976], pp. 69–93), Giorgio Magri has stated that *Avanti Urania!* dates from 1889. He also reports that the manuscript of the song is part of the collection of the composer's manuscripts at the Puccini museum at Torre del Lago.

2. This letter, quoted in part (in English only) by George R. Marek in *Puccini: A Biography* (New York: Simon and Schuster, 1951), is included in Gino Arrighi's "La corrispondenza di Giacomo Puccini con Maria Bianca Ginori Lisci" (in *Critica pucciniana*, p. 191), a collection of seventy letters and postcards that Puccini wrote to Marchese Ginori-Lisci's daughter.

3. According to *Lloyd's Register of British and Foreign Shipping* (London: 1895–1896), the *Urania* (Lloyd's entry No. 88) was originally built in 1879 by A. Hall & Co., Aberdeen, Scotland. Her port of registry under the Italian flag was Livorno.

Ginori's ancestors appended the maternal cognomen of Lisci to the family name.) Ginori-Lisci expanded the manufacturing, exportation, and popularization of porcelain, merging with the Società Ceramica (in 1896) to form the Società Ceramica Richard-Ginori, an international corporation active to the present day. He served in the Italian legislature and, in 1900, became a senator. He shared Puccini's passions for hunting, automobiles,[4] and music and provided the composer with welcome retreats at various private hunting estates, as well as a gift of the land at Torre del Lago, the site of the present Villa Puccini. At one time, a manuscript of *Le Villi* (1884), currently owned by the Mary Flagler Cary Music Collection in The Pierpont Morgan Library, New York City, was part of the Ginori family library. (It bears the bookplate "Ex Libris Petri Ginori Conti.") In 1896, Puccini dedicated the score of *La Bohème* to the Marchese. *Avanti Urania!* is dedicated to Marchese Ginori-Lisci's wife, the Marchesa Anna Ginori-Lisci.

The beginning of *Avanti Urania!* is similar to thematic material that Puccini later used in *Tosca* (1900):

Avanti Urania!

Tosca Act I

Tosca Act III

Some sections of *Avanti Urania!* anticipate the music associated with the heroine of *Madama Butterfly*.

Madama Butterfly—first version, 1904, Act I:

Part of *Avanti Urania!* is also reminiscent of the following theme from Puccini's *Preludio sinfonico* in A major, written while he was a student at the Milan Conservatory in 1882:

---

4. Marchese Ginori-Lisci is reported to have owned the first automobile imported into Italy.

(This *Preludio sinfonico* reputedly dates from 1876; however, the title page of the holograph full score is dated "Milano giugno 1882." At the end of the work, Puccini signed his name and added "Luglio 1882 Milano.")

The autograph manuscript of *Avanti Urania!* is now a part of the Paul Richards Manuscript Collection in the Mugar Library at Boston University. On the title page Puccini wrote: "Avanti Urania! / Parole di Renato Fucini / Musica di Giacomo Puccini / Torre del Lago / 4 ottobre '96." It consists of two pages of music (36 measures in a very neat hand) signed at the upper right-hand corner of the first page and again just below the last two measures. Also on the title page, in an unidentified hand, are the words "Autografo / del celebre maestro compositore / musicista Giacomo Puccini," written over two heavily abraded lines. The original words are not decipherable.

In 1899, *Avanti Urania!* was published in an edition for solo voice and piano by the Premiato Stabilimento Musicale Genesio Venturini in Florence and Rome (plate number 6904).[5] Earlier that year, Venturini brought out an edition of the *Inno a Diana*, composed in 1897; it bears an earlier plate number (6839) than that assigned to *Avanti Urania!* The Venturini edition differs slightly from the autograph; these variants are indicated in the present edition. All printings of the Venturini edition that I have seen bear the dedication "Alla Marchesa Anna Ginori Lisci"; however, no autograph dedication appears in the manuscript.

The text is by Puccini's frequent hunting companion Renato Fucini (b. 8 April 1843, Monterotondo Maritimo [Livorno]; d. 25 February 1921, Empoli) who, although considered one of the best of the Tuscan authors,[6] wrote reluctantly and only under the pressure of friends. Fucini graduated from the University of Pisa in 1863, having studied medicine and mathematics— both renounced for a diploma in agriculture and surveying. By 1865 he found himself paving streets and constructing sewers as an assistant engineer to the Commune of Florence. During this period, under the anagrammatic pseudonym of Neri Tanfuccio, he wrote a famous series of sonnets entitled *Cento sonetti in vernacolo pisano* (first published in 1872), which brought him notoriety (in the good sense of the word) in the salons of Florence and opened the doors to a new career in literature. Fucini's other works include *Napoli a occhio nudo* (1878); *Le veglie di Neri*, a collection of novellas and rustic tales (1884); *All'aria aperta* (1887); *Nella campagna toscana* (1908); *Poesie* (1920); children's stories in prose and verse, many of which were Fucini's translations of Russian and English tales; the autobiographical *Acqua passata* ("storielle e aneddoti della mia vita") (posthumously published in 1921); and *Foglie al vento* (1922).

On 6 January 1876, Fucini accepted the title of Cavaliere dell'Ordine della Corona d'Italia. He subsequently taught *belles letteres* and Italian at a boys' school in Pistoia, becoming, on 4 November 1879, the inspector of public schools there; on 19 December of that year he assumed that responsibility for all of the schools in the areas surrounding Pistoia. Like Puccini, Fucini was a welcome guest at Marchese Ginori-Lisci's private hunting estates at Montecristo and Torre del Lago. Fucini also wrote the text for Puccini's *E l'uccellino*.

---

5. Venturini published two different pictorial covers for his edition of *Avanti Urania!*: one with a photograph of the (actual?) steamer ship *Urania* (reproduced in *Mostra pucciniana*, Palazzo Provinciale di Lucca, 1974), and another with an engraving of a pleasure yacht in place of the photograph (copy: Library of Congress, received 12 February 1900). When the Milanese publisher Carisch & Jänichen acquired the firm, the song was reissued. The engraving on the cover was redone and additional pleasure yachts were added. There were no typographical alterations affecting the dedication, title headings, price, plate number, or date of publication in any of these printings.

6. An opinion shared by Carducci, Croce, D'Annunzio, Fogazzaro, Verga, and even Manzoni.

Avanti Urania! was not the only occasion for which Puccini provided music connected with a nautical vessel. The other was in honor of the launching of an Italian battleship at Sestri Ponente in Genoa. For this, Puccini supplied a *Movimento di valzer*—reputed to be the piece that he transformed into Musetta's Waltz. Originally written for solo piano, the *Movimento di valzer* was probably performed in an arrangement for military band or orchestra at the festivities held in conjunction with the launch. At the launching of the *Urania* under the Italian flag, *Avanti Urania!* may have been performed in an arrangement for band or voices and instruments made by someone other than Puccini.[7] However, as an intimate solo song, both the text and the music of *Avanti Urania!* clearly reveal Puccini's strong personal feelings of affection for Marchese Ginori-Lisci and the high esteem in which he held him.

---

7. It was not unusual for Puccini to entrust this task to a competent arranger, as was probably the case with another of his occasional instrumental pieces, the *Scossa elettrica*. It was certainly true of the *Inno a Roma*.

AVANTI *URANIA!*

Io non ho l'ali, eppur quando dal molo
Lancio la prora al mar,
Fermi gli alcioni sul potente volo
Si librano a guardar.

Io non ho pinne, eppur quando i marosi
Niun legno osa affrontar,
Trepidando, gli squali ardimentosi
Mi guardano passar!

Simile al mio signor,
Mite d'aspetto quanto è forte in cuor,
Le fiamme ho anch'io nel petto,
Anch'io di spazio,
Anch'io di gloria ho smania,
Avanti *Urania!!*

FORWARD *URANIA!*

I don't have wings, and yet when from the pier
I thrust my bow to sea,
The halcyons freeze in their potent flight as
They hover to watch.

I don't have fins, and yet when no other boat
Dares to brave the roaring seas,
Anxiously, the fearless sharks
Watch me go by!

Like my owner,
As mild in appearance as he is strong at heart,
I too have flames in my breast,
I too long for space,
I too crave glory,
Forward *Urania!!*

AVANTI *URANIA!*

Text by
RENATO FUCINI

Music by
GIACOMO PUCCINI
Edited by Michael Kaye

*The Venturini edition states: ♩ = 120.

dar. _____ Io non ho pin - ne, ep - pur quan-do i ma - ro - si

Niun le - gno o - sa af - fron - tar, _____ Tre - pi - dan - do, gli squa-li ar - di - men -

to - si Mi guar-da - no pas - sar! _____

Si - mi-le al mio si - gnor, _____ Mi - te d'a - spet - to quan-to è for-te in

67

* The Venturini edition gives the following reading:

INNO A DIANA

Text by Carlo Abeniacar

This song has often been confused with the *Inno a Roma*, composed in 1919.

PUCCINI'S DESCRIPTION of himself as a passionate hunter of waterfowl, good libretti, and beautiful women provides a revealing glimpse of the three main forces that dominated his life—sport, work, and sex. Hunting afforded him the opportunity to share the companionship of colleagues, collaborators, and artists; to take refuge from his domestic problems; and to cultivate the friendships of influential, well-connected members of privileged social stature who could, possibly, be useful to him. It also enabled him to mingle with and observe people from all walks of life who shared his love of the outdoors and his passions for shooting, boating, and spearfishing.[1]

The *capanno* Puccini referred to in his letter to Marchese Ginori-Lisci, dated 18 December 1895 (see page 61), was a favorite hunting site at Torre del Lago, the small town equidistant from Lucca, Pisa, and Viareggio, situated on Lake Massaciuccoli. "The lake was rich in water fowl. Swarms of moor-hens, wild duck, teal, divers, pheasants, and rooks made the region a veritable wild aviary. When the moon was out, the moor-hens rose. And Puccini took down his gun and jumped into the rowboat."[2] Torre del Lago became his happiest and most nearly permanent home. He maintained a villa there until 1921; today it is still preserved as a museum.

Torre del Lago was especially present in Puccini's thoughts when he traveled far from home, as the following undated letter to his friend Giovacchino Mazzini affirms:

Hotel Bristol, Wien I. Karnthnerring.

Caro Giovacchino, vicerè della banditissima.

Dalla città di Francesco invioti un saluto—il quale è un'ispirazione verso il verde Torre, che da lungi più bello appare agli occhi miei. O Malfante adorate, o fosse verdi e fetenti, ripiene di ranocchi melodiosi più della musica del grande di Lipsia—io vi amo e vi adoro—oramai siete sangue del mio sangue, siete organi necessari al mio essere.

Tuo aff.mo G. Puccini[3]

Hotel Bristol, Vienna I. Karnthnerring.

Dear Giovacchino, Viceroy of the Banditissima.

From Franz's city I send you a greeting—that expresses my longing for the green Torre which, from afar, seems even more beautiful to my eyes. Oh adored Malfante, oh green and smelly marshes filled with singing frogs more melodious than the music by the great one from Leipzig—I love you and adore you—you are by now the blood of my blood, you are organs indispensable to my being.

Your most affectionate G. Puccini[3]

---

1. An unsigned article in *Musical America* (22 December 1906) reports that Puccini was also a mountain climber and a wrestler.

2. The above description and the following letters from Giulio Ricordi to Puccini are excerpted from George R. Marek's *Puccini: A Biography*, pp. 132–33. For a first-hand account of Puccini's life at Torre del Lago, see Carlo Paladini's series of articles published in Ricordi's *Musica e Musicisti, Gazzetta Musicale di Milano* (Anno 58, Nos. 4 and 5, 1903), later augmented and revised as *Giacomo Puccini*.

3. Mario Puccioni, *Cacce e cacciatori di Toscana* (Florence: Vallecchi, 1934), p. 63.

Marchese Ginori-Lisci had granted Puccini the exclusive rights over all other hunters on Lake Massaciuccoli, and Puccini officiously signed his name to posters that read:

NOTICE TO HUNTERS

We hereby announce that the hunting season on Lake Massaciuccoli will open on the . . . day of. . . . Hunters are informed that the starting time is 11:00 A.M. and the hunt must close at sunset. Starting signals for the row boats will be fired at the following localities: Piaggetta, Gusciona and Torre del Lago. Admission 20 lire. Tickets may be purchased from special agents in the aforesaid localities.

Hunting is permitted on the lake and in the bushes, but is forbidden in the adjacent marshes. Hunters must show permits on request of the Carabinieri.

GIACOMO PUCCINI
Concessionaire [4]

In a letter dated 17 August 1893, Puccini's publisher, Giulio Ricordi, paternally admonished him:

But . . . the hunting season has begun!! Go easy, Puccini! Let your passion for the birds not seduce you away from music. . . . Therefore, one eye at the gunside but your thoughts at *Bohème*!

Later that year, on 12 October, Ricordi cautioned:

A little hunting is all right for a rest and for the refreshment of ideas, but afterwards I suggest that you also hunt the notes. . . . *Bohème* must surpass *Manon* and arrive at the right time.

Fortunately for Puccini, the score of *La Bohème* turned out to be of infinitely better quality than the music he wrote in praise of Diana.[5] But the *Inno a Diana* is not without merit. It begins in a spirited D major marchlike tempo, the theme of which is not unlike the energetic opening measures of the *Gloria* section of the so-called "Messa di Gloria":[6]

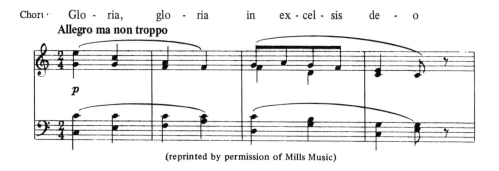

(reprinted by permission of Mills Music)

This mass also provided Puccini with music for another one of his intentional self-borrowings. The

---

4. Quoted in del Fiorentino, *Immortal Bohemian*, p. 92; pp. 89–96 of this book include several amusing accounts of Puccini's exploits as a hunter.

5. Diana was the Roman goddess of light, forests, and groves. Her Greek equivalent, Artemis, was more closely associated with hunting, fertility, and childbirth.

6. The correct title is simply *Messa a 4 Voci con Orchestra*. It was first performed on 12 July 1880 for the feast day of the patron saint of Lucca at the Church of San Paolino in that city. The *Credo* of this mass was originally written in 1878; the *Kyrie, Gloria, Sanctus, Benedictus,* and *Agnus Dei* date from 1880. The entire work is published by Belwin-Mills Publishing Corp., under the title "Messa di Gloria."

madrigal "Sulla vetta tu del monte," sung in Act II of *Manon Lescaut* (1893), was originally a setting of the *Agnus Dei*—an excellent, albeit incongruous use of preexisting material.

In the *Inno a Diana*, the music at the words "Tu li guida alle imprese più audaci" (measures 25–28) foreshadows that of Act I of *Tosca*, where, in the aria "Non la sospiri la nostra casetta," Tosca sings of the "nido a noi sacro, ignoto al mondo inter, pien d'amore e di mister." Perhaps in the opera Puccini was making a subconscious musical allusion to one of the private hunting retreats that his hobby provided.

Curiously, the first publication of the *Inno a Diana* was not, as is generally thought, in 1899 by the Florentine publisher Genesio Venturini. Rather, it first appeared in 1898 in an Italian magazine entitled *Sant'Uberto*.[7] This illustrated periodical, designed to appeal to hunters, was issued by Cavaliere G. Salvati in Naples. Venturini did bring out an edition of the song in 1899 (plate number 6839) with the dedication "Ai Cacciatori Italiani"; he also published an arrangement for brass band made by Bernardino Lanzi (plate number 6840).[8]

The autograph manuscript is part of the Frederick R. Koch Foundation Collection on deposit in The Pierpont Morgan Library in New York City. It consists of three pages, 71 measures (with numerous repeats, corrections, crossed out bars, and shorthand notations). It is signed and dated "12.12.[18]97"—hence the position of the *Inno a Diana* in this collection.

Carlo Abeniacar was an aficionado of hunting, a humorist, author, poet, painter, and sculptor. In 1877, the Florentine publisher O. Sersale brought out a collection of Abeniacar's writings entitled *A Caccia: profili e bozzetti*. His other works include *Lo Scorfano, esposizione umoristica di pittura e scultura: catalogo delle opere*, published in Naples in 1900. He was also an occasional photojournalist (see Abeniacar's article entitled "[Maxim] Gorki e [Roberto] Bracco a Capri" in *La Lettura*).[9] Abeniacar occasionally worked for Casa Ricordi versifying the Italian texts of Neapolitan songs.

On the cover of the issue of *Sant'Uberto* containing the *Inno a Diana* there is a reproduction of an autographed photograph of Puccini, dressed in elegant hunting attire, inscribed to Abeniacar and dated "25.2.[18]97."[10] The photograph also bears the following music in Puccini's hand:

Although this theme does not appear in the *Inno a Diana* (nor does it figure in the *Inno a Roma*), it was probably well known to the dedicatees of the song.

---

7. "Numero-Strenna Illustrato, 1898." Sant'Uberto is the patron saint of hunters, often invoked for protection against hydrophobia.

8. Hopkinson placed the Venturini edition of the *Inno a Diana* before *Avanti Urania!* because it bears an earlier plate number; however, he made no mention of its publication in *Sant'Uberto*, or of a version orchestrated by Vincenzo Billi (Carisch & Jänichen, 1919). Mosco Carner (*Puccini: A Critical Biography* [New York: Holmes & Meier, 1974], p. 117) confuses the *Inno a Diana* with the *Inno a Roma*, correctly dating the former from 1897 but incorrectly attributing the text to Fausto Salvatori (author of the words for the latter). Carner states that the *Inno a Diana* was composed for chorus and piano (an erroneous conclusion he also makes when describing *Avanti Urania!*). Other writers have mistakenly called the *Inno a Roma* a re-elaboration of the *Inno a Diana*.

9. Published by the *Corriere della Sera*, Milan, December 1910, pp. 1136–40.

10. Puccini mentioned Abeniacar in at least two letters to Tito Ricordi. See Letters 28 and 29 in *Puccini: 276 lettere inedite*, Giuseppe Pintorno, ed. (Milan: Nuove Edizioni, 1974).

A Recipe from Puccini's Kitchen

Folaghe alla "Puccini"

Si spellano le Folaghe, anzi che pelarle: se mettono nell'acqua fresca per un' ora, o un'ora e mezzo; quindi si tagliano a pezzi e si mettono al fuoco in una casseruola, con sale, pepe o peperone rosso, pochissimo olio, sedano, carote e cipolla (in abbondanza) un poco di basilico, maggiorana, gnebitella (mentuccia) e lauro.

Si copre la casseruola e si fanno cuocere lentamente per circa un'ora: dopo si scuopre la casseruola facendole cuocere alla svelta finchè siano colorite. Dopo la coloritura ci si mette un bicchiere di acqua con poco vino; e quando questo liquido è assorbito ci si metta un poco di brodo, si cuoprono e si fanno cuocere lentamente per mezz'ora, dopo averci messo un po' di farina per far rapprendere la salsa. La salsa poi si passa per setaccio e si può servire coi crostini.

GIACOMO PUCCINI

In 1903, Puccini had the above recipe typed. He signed and mailed it from Torre del Lago to his friends and associates. In English it reads:

Coots "Puccini" Style

Pluck, do not skin, the coots; cover them with cold water for one or one-and-a-half hours; then cut them up and put them into a pot on the fire. Add salt, black or red pepper, very little oil, celery, carrots and lots of onions, a little basil, marjoram, mint, and bay leaf.

Cover the pot and let them cook slowly for about one hour: then uncover the pot and quickly brown the coots; then add a glass of water with a little bit of wine. When this liquid has been absorbed, a little stock is added. The pot is again covered and they are cooked slowly for half an hour longer, after having added a bit of flour to thicken the sauce. The sauce is then strained and the dish can be served with toasted bread.

GIACOMO PUCCINI

Courtesy of the Pierpont Morgan Library.*

Another manuscript of this song exists. An autograph fair copy (also dated 12 December 1887), bearing a lengthy dedication to Abeniacar, was sold at Sotheby's on 6 May 1981. It is now in a private collection and was unavailable for collation with the manuscript pictured here.

---

*Another manuscript of this song exists. An autograph fair copy (also dated 12 December 1887), bearing a lengthy dedication to Abeniacar, was sold at Sotheby's on 6 May 1981. It is now in a private collection and was unavailable for collation with the manuscript pictured here.

INNO A DIANA

Ai Cacciatori Italiani

Gloria a te, se alle notti silenti
Offri, o Cinzia,* i bei raggi all'amor;
Gloria a te, se ai meriggi cocenti
Tempri, o Diana, dei forti il valor.

Sui tuoi baldi e fedeli seguaci
Veglia sempre con l'occhio divin;
Tu li guida alle imprese più audaci,
Li sorreggi nell'aspro cammin.

Dalle vette dell'Alpi nevose
Fino ai lidi del siculo mar;
Per i campi el le selve più ombrose,
Dove amavi le fiere incontrar;

Sovra i laghi, ove baciano l'onda
Le corolle di candidi fior,

Giunga a te, come un'eco profonda,
Questo fervido canto d'amor!

Gloria a te, Gloria, Gloria!

HYMN TO DIANA

Dedicated to Italian Hunters

Glory to you, O Cynthia,* when in the silent nights
You offer the beautiful rays to love;
Glory to you, O Diana, when in the hot afternoons
You strengthen the courage of the brave ones.

Always watch over your fearless and faithful followers
With your divine eye;
Guide them to the most daring undertakings,
Sustain them on the rough pathway.

From the peaks of the snowy Alps
To the shores of the Sicilian sea,
Through the fields and the shadiest woods,
Where you loved to meet the wild animals;

Over the lakes, where the petals of white flowers
Kiss the wave,

May this fervent song of love reach you
Like a joyous echo.

Glory to you, Glory, Glory!

---

* Cinzia, or Cynthia (a Roman epithet of Diana), was the goddess of the moon, believed to have been born on Mount Cynthus, the birthplace of Apollo and Artemis.

"Ai Cacciatori Italiani"

INNO A DIANA

Text by
CARLO ABENIACAR

Music by
GIACOMO PUCCINI
Edited by Michael Kaye

* The indications in parentheses appear only in the Venturini edition.

* In measures 29 and 30 of the Venturini edition the bass is marked staccato.

Dal - le vet - te del - l'Al - pi ne - vo - se Fi - no ai li - di del

si - cu - lo mar; Per i cam - pi e le sel - ve più om - bro - se,__

Do - ve a - ma - vi le fie - re in - con - trar;_____

I° Tempo

So - vra i la - ghi, o - ve ba - cia - no l'on - da Le co - rol - le di

* "gioconda" in the Venturini edition.

E L'UCCELLINO, Ninna-Nanna

Text by Renato Fucini

THIS ENTRANCING, WISTFUL lullaby, with its playful piano accompaniment, is perhaps the best-known Puccini song. It was composed at Torre del Lago in 1899. Published that same year by G. Ricordi & C., it was advertised in the *Gazzetta Musicale di Milano* of 8 February 1900 as a song for mezzo-soprano or baritone.

E l'uccellino was written as a cradle song for the infant son of one of Puccini's closest friends, Guglielmo Lippi, a respected physician in Lucca who had died in 1897 of a typhus infection a few days after his marriage to the Countess Nelda Prosperi. The baby, born in 1898, was nicknamed Memmo.[1] In the absence of his own father, he was treated almost like an adopted child by another one of Puccini's good friends, Alfredo Caselli (who organized a memorial tribute to Guglielmo Lippi, Sr., in the form of an album of writings contributed by Dr. Lippi's Lucca friends). On 28 July 1898, Puccini sent the following letter to the poet Giovanni Pascoli:

Gentilissimo Sig. Professore

Uniscomi alla desolata famiglia Lippi, all'amico Alfredo Caselli di Lucca per pregarla a voler dettare un' epigrafe per il mio povero amico Guglielmo Lippi.

Ella, colla elettissima forma e coll'animo suo gentile potrà in poche parole esprimere i sentimenti di noi tutti verso il disgraziato giovane.

Voglia scusarmi per la libertà che mi sono presa—e mi tenga per suo ammiratore e devoto servo

Giacomo Puccini

Most gracious Professor,

I join the grieved Lippi family and my friend Alfredo Caselli of Lucca in begging you to compose an epigraph for my late friend Guglielmo Lippi.

You, with your elegant style and out of the goodness of your heart, will be able to express in few words the sentiment of all of us toward the unfortunate young man.

Please forgive me for taking this liberty—and believe me your admirer and devoted servant.

Giacomo Puccini[2]

This song, which Puccini originally intended as an intimate and heartfelt present to the bereaved Lippi family, became a favorite recital piece. The first edition of *E l'uccellino* bore the dedication "Al bimbino MEMMO LIPPI." It was translated into German by Louise Perrot (as *Das Vögelchen*, 1915) and into English by Lute Drummond (as A *Little Birdie, Lullaby*, 1919). In April 1920, it was reprinted in the musical supplement to Ricordi's magazine *Musica d'oggi* (Anno 2, No. 4). In 1924 it was also scored by Vincenzo Billi[3] for a small orchestra and was published in at least three keys (the first edition was in D major). *E l'uccellino* has been recorded several times, first by

---

1. Memmo (also known as Memmino) Lippi's first name was actually Guglielmo; he later adopted his stepfather's name of Francesconi. He became a psychiatrist and the director of a mental institution in Lucca. He was deported and killed by the Nazis in 1944.

2. Included in Gino Arrighi's "Caleidoscopio di umanità in lettere di Giacomo Puccini" in *Giacomo Puccini nel centenario della nascita* (Lucca: Rassegna del Comune, Anno II, No. 4, September 1958).

3. The composer-conductor Vincenzo Billi (b. 4 April 1869, Brisighella [Romagna]; d. 20 February 1938, Florence) also orchestrated the *Inno a Diana*. Puccini is the dedicatee of Billi's successful song *Ventaglio*.

the mezzo-soprano Armida Parsi-Pettinella (for Fonotipia, 1908), and subsequently by Licia Albanese (with orchestra, 1954), Marcella Reale (1974), and Renata Tebaldi (1974). It is well suited for recitalists and opera singers alike.

Renato Fucini also wrote the text for *Avanti Urania!* On 22 February 1921, when Fucini was ill and dying in Empoli, Puccini wrote to the author and publicist Carlo Paladini:

> . . . Da tutte le parti arrivano a me a Ricordi e Sonzogno lettere telg: chiedendo notizie mia salute - Perchè la telefonata da Empoli per il povero Fucini, aggravatissimo . . . fu interpretata e intesa: Puccini invece di Fucini -E la notizia ha girato il mondo - Bisognerà dire che sto bene? Crepi l'astrologo.

> . . . Ricordi, Sonzogno, and I get letters and telegrams from everywhere asking for news of my health - Because the telephone call from Empoli for the poor and very ill Fucini . . . was interpreted and understood as Puccini instead of Fucini, and the news traveled around the world. Will it be necessary to say that I am well? Damn the astrologer.[4]

---

4. Paladini, *Giacomo Puccini*, Letter No. 42.

E L'UCCELLINO

E l'uccellino canta sulla fronda:
Dormi tranquillo, boccuccia d'amore;
Piegala giù quella testina bionda,
Della tua mamma posala sul cuore.

E l'uccellino canta su quel ramo,
Tante cosine belle imparerai,
Ma se vorrai conoscer quant'io t'amo,
Nessuno al mondo potrà dirlo mai!

E l'uccellino canta al ciel sereno:
Dormi tesoro mio qui sul mio seno.

AND THE LITTLE BIRD

And the little bird sings on the leafy branch:
Sleep peacefully, little love;
Put down your little blond head,
Rest it upon your mamma's heart.

And the little bird sings upon that leafy branch:
You will learn many pretty things,
But if you want to know how much I love you,
No one in the world will ever be able to tell you!

And the little bird sings in the clear sky:
Sleep my treasure here upon my breast.

E L'UCCELLINO

(Ninna–Nanna)

Text by
RENATO FUCINI

Music by
GIACOMO PUCCINI
Edited by Michael Kaye

CANTO

PIANOFORTE

E l'uc - cel -

li - no can - ta sul - la fron - da: Dor - mi tran -

quil - lo, boc - cuc - cia d'a - mo - re; Pie - ga - la giù quel - la te -

poco rit. a tempo

sti - na bion - da, Del - la tua mam - ma po - sa - la sul

poco rit. a tempo

cuo - re. E l'uc - cel - li - no

can - ta su quel ra - mo, Tan - te co - si - ne

poco rall.

poco rall.

a tempo dolce e carezzevole

bel - le im - pa - re - ra - i, Ma se vor - rai co - no - scer quan - t'io

a tempo

83

poco rit. a tempo

t'a - mo, Nes - su - no al mon - do po - trà dir - lo ma - i!

poco rit. a tempo

pp

E l'uc - cel - li - no can - ta al ciel se -

rall.

re - no: Dor - mi te - so - ro mio qui sul mio

rall.

rit. a tempo

se - no.

rit. a tempo rall.

84

TERRA E MARE

Text by Enrico Panzacchi

IN 1901, EDOARDO DE FONSECA founded the "Albo Annuale d'Arti e Lettere" ("Annual Album of Arts and Letters"), which he called *Novissima*. The debut issue was an incontestable critical and artistic success, garnering from newspapers and major periodicals such plaudits as "a battle fought and won in the cause of Italian culture" (*Fieramosca*, Florence); "this worthy artistic publication arrives just in time to disperse the proliferation of mediocre risible writings that make their inevitable appearance between Christmas and New Years" (*Il Marzocco*, Florence); "never in Italy has there been such a terse, refined and, above all, well-conceived publication as this *Novissima*" (*Corriere Italiano*, Milan); "which to a great degree endeavors to refine the taste of the entire nation" (*Nuova Antologia*, Florence); "with a correctness, diligence and admirable good taste" (*Il Resto del Carlino*, Bologna). De Fonseca was also personally commended for his initiative in this undertaking. In striving to produce a high quality publication he sought artwork, poetry, writings, polychromes, and music from the brushes and pens of (in his words) "Italy's most original contemporary artists, composers, and leading literary figures." The impressive list of contributing artists and writers included Leonardo Bistolfi, Giacomo Grosso, Lorenzo Delleani, Clemente Pugliese, A. Tominetti, Alfredo Galli, Pio Joris, Arturo Noci, Ettore de Maria, and Giorgio Belloni (artists); and Antonio Fogazzaro, Gabriele D'Annunzio, Edmond De Amicis, Giovanni Pascoli, Giuseppe Giacosa, Renato Fucini, Arturo Colautti, and Amilcare Solferini (writers).[1]

De Fonseca invited Puccini, Alberto Franchetti, Umberto Giordano, and Carlo Cordara to compose music especially for *Novissima*. The predominant theme of the 1902 issue was the sea: "We thought it good to dedicate a considerable part of our second publication to a special subject, *The Sea*, by inviting the major authors and artists of our country to express their thoughts on this grand topic." Puccini's contribution was the impressionistic vignette entitled *Terra e mare*, to a poem of the same name by Enrico Panzacchi, a leading Bolognese critic and ardent Wagnerian,[2] who was an important figure in Italian cultural life.

Terra e mare was published in *Novissima 1902* along with a facsimile of Puccini's autograph manuscript reproduced in miniature on the title page of the music. The manuscript is signed and dated "Torre del Lago / 3 [October?] 1902." Beginning at measure 20, the music in the manuscript differs from that in the published version. Both versions are given in this collection.

Each of the four oblong pages of the *Novissima 1902* edition of *Terra e mare* is printed with a decorative border depicting land- and seascapes. In that publication, the song is preceded by D'Annunzio's poem entitled *Le Ore* (written in 1900). It is followed by a poem by Arturo Colautti (the librettist of Giordano's *Fedora* [1898] and Cilèa's *Adriana Lecouvreur* [1902] and *Gloria* [1907]).[3]

---

1. In the second year of publication, the list of contributors numbered fifty-six artists and forty-six writers.

2. Panzacchi reported on the first Bayreuth Festival for *Nuova Antologia* (2nd series, III, 10 October 1876, pp. 265–78).

3. Puccini attempted to collaborate with D'Annunzio (1863–1938) several times, and once with Colautti (1851–1914), but could not seem to arrive at mutually acceptable subjects for opera libretti.

Enrico Panzacchi (b. 16 December 1840, Ozzano d'Emilia; d. 5 October 1904, Bologna) received his early education in a seminary and went on to graduate from the University of Pisa with a degree in philology. In 1866, he was appointed a professor of history at the Liceo di Sassari, and four years later (after the publication of his discourse entitled *Arte moderna*), he became a professor of philosophy at the University of Bologna. He subsequently taught art history and aesthetics at the Accademia di Belle Arti—an institution he eventually served as president. Panzacchi was an accomplished art historian, lecturer, and critic whose numerous literary and poetical works were well respected, as were his views on music, philosophy, and aesthetics.

Panzacchi was also a dedicated public servant. As secretary of education for the municipality of Bologna and the surrounding provinces (ca. 1868), he is credited with the improvement of the Bolognese elementary schools and other civic and cultural institutions in that city. Recognizing that students attending the public schools were lacking in instruction in areas of cultural awareness, he ordered all teachers to include lessons in art history. When many of them complained that they were unequipped to impart these studies to their students, Panzacchi saw to it that these teachers received training and teaching aids (including photographs and lesson plans covering painting, sculpture, and architecture). He was known in some circles as "il sognatore ambulante" ("the ambulant dreamer"). A long-lasting result of Panzacchi's tenure as secretary of education was the secularization of Bologna's public schools, thus returning religious instruction to homes and churches, where it remained until 1895. Panzacchi's rational anticlerical posture is still remembered in that city. He was a skillful orator capable of influencing public opinion. His *Ode alla Regina* earned him fame and recognition throughout Italy.

The definitive edition of Panzacchi's collected poetry is published in two volumes, the first entitled *Visioni e immagini*, and the second, *Alma natura* (1894).[4] Many of his lyrical poems were assigned to Italian schoolchildren for memorization and recitation. Panzacchi's works include *Piccolo romanziere* (1872), *Lyrica, romanze e canzoni* (1877–1882), *Vecchio ideale* (1879), *Racconti e liriche* (1882), *Ricardo Wagner, ricordi e studi* (1883), *Nel mondo della musica, impressioni e ricordi* (1895), *Nel campo dell'arte, assaggi di critica* (1897), *Nuove liriche* (1888), *Rime novelle* (1898), and *Cor sincerum* (1902). A collection of his prose was posthumously published in 1913. The poem *Terra e mare* is the sixteenth entry in section fifteen of Panzacchi's *Ultime rime*.[5]

Re Edoardo de Fonseca, see [*Casa mia, casa mia*], page 115.

---

4. In 1908, Giovanni Pascoli edited Panzacchi's poetry for the Bolognese publisher Nicola Zanichelli; a second edition was printed in 1910.

5. The poem is undated, but it was probably written ca. 1901–1902; see Zanichelli's second edition of Panzacchi's poetry (Bologna, 1910, p. 519).

TERRA E MARE

I pioppi, curvati dal vento,
Rimugghiano in lungo filare.
Dal buio, tra il sonno, li sento
E sogno la voce del mar.

E sogno la voce profonda
Dai placidi ritmi possenti;
Mi guardan, specchiate dall'onda,
Le stelle nel cielo fulgenti.

Ma il vento più forte tempesta,
De' pioppi nel lungo filare,
Dal sonno giocondo mi desta...
Lontana è la voce del mar!

EARTH AND SUN

The long rows of poplars, bent by the wind,
Are roaring again.
In the darkness, half asleep, I hear them
And I dream of the voice of the sea.

And I dream of the deep voice
With its peaceful, mighty rhythms;
Reflected in the wave, the stars shining in the sky
Are looking at me.

But the wind rages louder
Through the row of poplars,
It wakes me from my joyous sleep...
Distant is the voice of the sea!

TERRA E MARE

Text by
ENRICO PANZACCHI

a) Version according to the autograph
First Edition

Music by
GIACOMO PUCCINI
Edited by Michael Kaye

*Puccini chose not to retain Panzacchi's rhyme of "filare" and "mare."

guar - dan, spec-chia - te dal - l'on - da, Le stel - le nel cie - lo ful - gen - ti.

Ma il ven - to più for - te tem - pe - sta, De'

piop - pi nel lun-go fi - la - re, Dal son - no gio-con-do mi de - sta... Lon -

ta - na è la vo - ce del mar!

TERRA E MARE

Text by
ENRICO PANZACCHI

b) Published version

Music by
GIACOMO PUCCINI
Edited by Michael Kaye

guar - dan, spec-chia-te dal - l'on - da, Le stel - le nel cie - lo ful - gen - ti.

Ma il ven - to più for - te tem - pe - sta, De'

piop - pi nel lun - go fi - la - re, Dal son - no gio-con - do mi de - sta... Lon -

ta-na è la vo - ce del mar! _

London, 1907.

Berlin, 1913.

CANTO D'ANIME, Pagina d'album

Text by Luigi Illica

CANTO D'ANIME WAS written by Puccini expressly for the gramophone. It was commissioned by Alfred Michaelis for the Gramophone Company (Italy), Ltd. The background of that commission and the events surrounding the composition, publication, and subsequent recording of *Canto d'anime* provide a fascinating glimpse of the European recording industry in its early years. The following chronicle is based largely on documents generously provided by the EMI Music Archives. It also illustrates Puccini's views on early copyright law, composers' royalties, and the phonograph.

On 13 September 1899, the Gramophone Company Limited (London) engaged Alfred Michaelis to head the newly established Milan office of the Gramophone Company (Italy), Ltd. In his capacity as manager of the Italian subsidiary, Michaelis was virtually given carte blanche by the parent company. In addition to a handsome salary and an expense account, he also held 4,417 shares of stock in the Italian company valued at one pound each.

> According to the agreements made at the foundation of the Co. I was named Manager for the Northern part of Italy, & my brother for the Southern part.[1]

Believing Alfred to be more reliable and more conservative than his brother,[2] the managing director of the London office, William Barry Owen, established the following mode of procedure for operations in Italy in a letter to the Michaelis brothers dated 7 November 1900:

> Mr. Alfred Michaelis will undertake the full and entire responsibility of the affairs in Italy. There will be, for the time being, no bank account kept except by Mr. Alfred Michaelis in Italy, which bank account he will have made in the name of the "Gramophone Company (Italy) Limited" and it will be subject to his Cheque as Manager. If Mr. Alfred Michaelis sees fit that Mr. William Michaelis shall open an account in the name of the "Gramophone Company (Italy), Limited" at Naples, and conduct it in the same way he is at perfect liberty to do so. . . .
>
> The real point that we wish you to understand is that we are putting the whole of the success in this business into your hands fully and without reserve, and that for the time being we do not care to receive any reports from you whatever.

Alfred Michaelis became a well-known and controversial figure in Italian musical life. He was instrumental in making the first recordings in the Vatican, and he successfully negotiated with Enrico Caruso and other golden age singers to make important records—including the famous recordings that Caruso made at the Grand Hotel in Milan in March of 1902 and those of Francesco Tamagno, recorded at the tenor's home in 1903. Michaelis was the first record producer to regularly employ a small orchestra to provide the accompaniment for recordings of operatic music. He dreamed of being able to record live performances at La Scala.

---

1. Excerpt from a letter from Alfred Michaelis to William Barry Owen, dated 18 January 1900. Unless otherwise stated, the original documents and correspondence quoted in these notes are in the EMI Music Archives, Hayes (Middlesex, England). The English translations are those of certain anonymous Gramophone & Typewriter Company (G & T) employees, who were very inconsistent in their use of "Ltd." and "Limited."

2. William Michaelis, of Brighton, headed the Naples office of the Gramophone Company (Italy), Ltd. He is credited with the invention of the Neophone in 1904.

While he was composing *Madama Butterfly*, Puccini evidently contacted Michaelis:

22nd Jan. 1903

W. B. Owen Esq.
    Gramophone & Typewriter Ltd.
       L O N D O N

Dear Sir,

    Giacomo Puccini, the composer who has given us the letter about which I wrote you yesterday, is writing a new opera on the Japanese subject, taken from an English operetta [*sic*], *Madame Butterfly*. For this opera which the musical world is impatiently expecting and which will be at once represented at the "Metropolitan" at New York[3] and certainly in London too, he requires Japanese music, and as he knows through me that Gaisberg is in Japan he has asked me as a favour to let him have as quickly as possible the Japanese records taken. Have you got them? Anyhow do your utmost to let me have them with the least delay possible, as he said yesterday while working at his opera that he was very sorry he could not have them at this very moment.

    I need not point out to you the extreme importance of the Gramo[phone] becoming a necessary instrument for composers. It is difficult for Puccini to go to Japan to study Japanese music. Well, the Gramophone brings Japan to his house.

    I have rendered a similar service to Umberto Giordano, the composer of *Fedora*, *Andrea Chénier*, etc., who has asked me for Russian choruses which he required to study for his new opera *Siberia* which will be represented at the Scala next winter. Please do <u>not</u> use this information in the meantime for advertisement—it is too early and the subject is very delicate.

    ADVERTISING—I am now preparing a large placard with the Hollow arm and the names of Tamagno, De Lucia and Caruso. Under the machine, are the following autographs (extracts from autograph letters):

"Meraviglioso"
    Umberto Giordano
"Gioiello artistico"
    Francesco Cilèa

"Insuperabile"
    Arturo Toscanini
"Prezioso"
    Ruggero Leoncavallo

"Delizioso"
Giacomo Puccini

thus we are advertising Tamagno's, De Lucia's and Caruso's machine signed by all the great composers.

Yours very truly,
A. Michaelis

    The enterprising Michaelis was responsible for commissioning Puccini to write a song "espressamente per il Grammofono" ("expressly for the Gramophone"). Michaelis also invited Franchetti, Giordano, Leoncavallo, and Mascagni to compose songs for the Gramophone Company (Italy), Ltd. They enthusiastically accepted the opportunity, but Puccini was reluctant to participate in the project. Michaelis nagged him until he finally agreed to write something, and in April 1903 Puccini signed the following contract:

---

3. The Metropolitan Opera première of *Madama Butterfly* did not occur until 11 February 1907.

Agreement
Maestro Giacomo Puccini.
(MILAN)
Song.

Milan 15th April 1903

Between the Maestro Giacomo Puccini, master of music, and Mr. Alfred Michaelis, Manager of the Gramophone Company (Italy), Ltd, of Milan, the following agreement is established:

1st. The Maestro Giacomo Puccini binds himself to write a Song for one voice, for exclusive reproduction on the Gramophone or other talking machines; the publication, printed or by any other means, is strictly forbidden, unless with the special permission of the Gramophone Company (Italy), Ltd.

2nd. The Maestro Giacomo Puccini declares herewith that he cedes all the Author's rights on said song for Italy and abroad to the Gramophone Company (Italy), Ltd.

3rd. Mr. Michaelis on his part engages to compensate the Maestro Giacomo Puccini with one thousand Discs (1,000) to be chosen by the Maestro Giacomo Puccini.

4th. The above mentioned Song to be written and consigned to the Gramophone Company (Italy), Ltd, within the space of two months from the date of this present contract.

Signed: Giacomo Puccini.
Alfred Michaelis.

Luigi Illica wrote the verses for Puccini's song for the Gramophone Company. They were written specifically for the occasion and at the composer's request. This is documented in certain as yet unpublished letters exchanged between Puccini and the poet, as well as in three of the more obscure letters found in the *Carteggi pucciniani*. On 27 April 1903, Puccini wrote to Illica:

> Venne Cottone col foglio dei mille e firmai. Tu prepara piccole spavalde o languide strofe (due in tutto), non conviene conceder tanto a chi paga così male. Ma dimmi, non è il caso, data la noia che genera il grammofono, di fare una società per la vendita dei dischi a ribasso? Vero che questa proposta avrebbe dovuto sorgere da Franchetti, ma chi sa che non abbia già fatto affari colla gatta nel sacco?!

> Cottone came with the contract for the one thousand [records] and I signed.[4] You prepare short, haughty, or languid stanzas (two in all); there is no advantage in giving too much to somebody who pays so badly. Tell me, wouldn't it be a good idea, given the boredom generated by the gramophone, to start a business to sell records at discount prices? It is true that such a proposition should have come from Franchetti, but who knows, maybe he has done it already and has the cat in the bag?![5]

---

4. Puccini was probably referring to the contract of 15 April 1903. Salvatore Cottone was the accompanist for Caruso's recordings made at the Grand Hotel.

5. Eugenio Gara, ed., *Carteggi pucciniani* (Milan: Ricordi, 1958), p. 255, n. 1.

On 14 May 1903, Michaelis telegraphed the London office:

"Puccini requires urgently Japanese records please solicit."

Michaelis received the following letter in reply:

May 14th 1903

In answer to your telegram concerning Japanese Records, I am very sorry to say we have had a bad piece of news. Today we hear that the steamer, on which the originals of the Japanese Records were shipped, has arrived in the docks in London, and reports a fire on board, and, in all probability, our Records are all lost. I do not know this is true yet, or in what condition they are, and we are hoping against hope that they will come out all right. I will let you know about it as soon as it is possible.

Yours faithfully,

THE GRAMOPHONE & TYPEWRITER LTD
Managing Director

The Japanese recordings eventually reached Puccini by the fall of 1903. In an interview with the composer published in *Musical America* on 26 January 1907, Puccini stated, "I had phonograph records of Japanese music sent to me, and many of the themes I have employed in the score of *Madama Butterfly*, changing them very little."

On 25 February 1903, Puccini was injured in an automobile accident en route home from a visit to Alfredo Caselli's. The accident left him with a limp for the rest of his life and he was forced to endure a slow and painful recovery. This, complicated by the fact that he learned he had diabetes, resulted in a delay in completing work on *Madama Butterfly*. It also kept Puccini from fulfilling his promise to write a song for Michaelis. In June 1903, Puccini wrote to Illica, who had apparently already supplied two unsuitable texts for the song:

Bisogna che tu ti armi di pazienza e me ne faccia una terza. *Omne trinum*. . . . Ed ecco perchè. Lirica, no. A soggetto, neppure. Dunque? La canzonetta a *couplet* è quel che ci vuole, così anche il sor Giulio [Ricordi] vedrà che noi si è fatto una burletta e il pubblico lo stesso. Una canzonetta un po' lascivetta che potrebbe cantarsi da qualche Cantalamessa qualunque, a tempo di marcia uso la *Francesa* di Costa—e quella la spiffero subito senza fatica.

You have to arm yourself with patience and prepare a third one for me. *Omne trinum*. . . . And here is why. Not a lyrical one, or a topical one. Then what? What is needed here is a *couplet* for the little song. This way both Mr. Giulio [Ricordi] and the public will take it for what it is: a little joke. A song that is a bit lascivious, one that could be sung by any Cantalamessa, with a marching beat like *Francesa* by Costa—something like that I can turn out quickly without difficulty.[6]

One week before the première of the first version of *Madama Butterfly*, Puccini wrote to Illica in Castell'Arquato:

---

6. Quoted in ibid. Reference in last sentence is to Pasquale Mario Costa (b. 1858, Taranto; d. 1933, Monte Carlo).

Milano, 10 febbraio 1904

Caro Illica,

è qui il "grammofono" in seduta a reclamare il parto mio! Mandami due o tre strofe ritmiche con concetto che finisca colla fine del verso. Per carità non "aurora." C'è Franchetti e Leone-Cavallo che cantano più o meno tenebrosamente lo nascente sole. Mandami dunque un pensiero passionale poetico magari lunare per tenore (per Caruso). I "grammofonitt" fremono e ne hanno bisogno ed io voglio uscirne. Le prove bene, ma . . . Vieni?

Milan, 10 February 1904

Dear Illica,

"Gramophone"[7] is here to demand the fruit of my labor! Send me two or three rhythmical verses with a concept that ends at the end of the verse. But please not "aurora" ["dawn"]. Both Franchetti and Leone-Cavallo sing, more or less in dark moods, of the rising sun. So please send me a poetic, passionate thought, perhaps a lunar one, for tenor (for Caruso). The "record makers" are all stammering that they want it, and I want out of it. The rehearsals [for *Madama Butterfly*] are going well, but . . . Are you coming?[8]

Illica had written the text for Franchetti's *romanza*, entitled *Verso l'aurora*, destined for the Gramophone Company. Leoncavallo provided Michaelis with what would prove to be the very successful song *Mattinata*, which begins "L'aurora di bianco vestito." (Mascagni's and Giordano's contributions are listed below.) Illica obviously took Puccini at his word, for the last line of the *Canto d'anime* is "a sfidar l'oblio l'odio la morte dove non son tenèbre e tutto è sol!"

Michaelis was impatient to receive Puccini's song, which was almost one year overdue. In March of 1904, the bass-baritone Enrico Berriel wrote the following puzzling correspondence to Michaelis on the Gramophone Company (Italy), Ltd., letterhead. (The first letter was originally in French, the second in Italian.)[9]

Milan, 19 March 1904

Dear Sir,

I am in receipt of your esteemed letter of today, and I confirm to you that it expresses exactly the verbal conventions concluded between us. I enclose herewith the receipt of the sum of Frs. 500 (five hundred francs) for travelling expenses and I undertake to go to Paris within the current of next week in order to take immediate steps. I give you my word of honour that I shall maintain the most absolute secrecy with regard to the mission with which you have trusted me. The obligations are taken in the name of Madame de Marsan and myself respectively.

Yours, etc.
Henri Berriel

---

7. Probably a nickname for Michaelis.

8. *Carteggi pucciniani*, Letter No. 346, p. 255. In 1893, when Puccini and Ruggero Leoncavallo were at odds over the duplication of effort concerning the composition of *La Bohème*, Puccini referred to the author of *Pagliacci* as "Leonasino" and "Leonbestia"; here he calls him "Lion-Horse."

9. In 1904, Enrico (better known as Enrique) Berriel recorded for the G & T label, accompanied on the piano by Salvatore Cottone. Like Cottone, Berriel also acted as an intermediary for Michaelis.

Milan, 21 March 1904

I beg to acknowledge receipt of the original contract, dated April 15, 1903, concluded between you and Mo. Giacomo Puccini for a *Romanza* which the latter requested me to write for you. The said contract was given to me in confidence, in order to facilitate for me the work proposed, on the 19th [of this month], and I am bound to restore it to you, at your request, and in any case at the conclusion of my mission.

Yours faithfully,
Enrico Berriel

[PS:] From 30/3 to 2/5 Teatro del Liceo, Barcelona[10]

The significance of Berriel's letters remains unclear.

Michaelis secured the services of the Officine Grafiche D. Coen & C. in Milan to provide the necessary musical typography services, and, in 1904, the Italian branch of the Gramophone Company began publishing the compositions they also planned to record. On 23 December 1904, the Library of Congress received copies of the following songs, all published by the Gramophone Company (Italy), Ltd., and printed in Milan:

> "*Ascoltiamo!* Romanza per Canto con Accompagnamento di Piano composta sopra poesia originale di Guido Menasci. Da Pietro Mascagni, scritta espressamente pel Grammofono";
>
> "*Canto d'Anime*, Pagina d'Album scritta espressamente per il Grammofono. Poesia di Luigi Illica, Musica di Giacomo Puccini";
>
> "*Verso l'Aurora*, Romanza per Tenore. Poesia di Luigi Illica. Musica di Alberto Franchetti scritta espressamente pel Grammofono";
>
> "*Mattinata*. Per voce di Tenore o Soprano. Parole e Musica di Ruggiero [*sic*] Leoncavallo. Scritta espressamente pel Grammofono"; and
>
> "*Crepuscolo Triste*. Romanza per Mezzo-soprano. Composta espressamente per il Grammofono. Poesia di Romeo Carugati. Musica di Umberto Giordano. Riduzione per Canto e Pianoforte."

On 2 May 1904, Puccini signed the following important contract with Michaelis, which unfortunately was destined never to be fulfilled:

M° Giacomo Puccini
Conducting Milan

Between the Maestro GIACOMO PUCCINI and Mr. ALFRED MICHAELIS the Manager of the Gramophone Company (Italy), Ltd., the following agreement is established:

1st – The Maestro Puccini engages and binds himself to musically arrange and direct all the vocal and instrumental productions ["esecuzioni"] that Mr. Michaelis in his quality as Manager of the Gramophone Company desires privately to record on the Discs of the Gramophone.

In remuneration for the above mentioned, Mr. Michaelis binds himself to compensate the Maestro in the following manner.

---

10. In 1900, Berriel had appeared in New Orleans; in the spring of 1904, he made his debut in Barcelona, where he sang Le Père in *Louise* (on opening night), the title role in *Rigoletto*, and Telramund in *Lohengrin*.

For the musical arranging and directing of a Song with pianoforte accompaniment Liras 200 (two hundred)

With orchestral accompaniment Liras 300 (three hundred)

For a Symphonic or Choral piece Liras 400 (four hundred)

For each complete act of an Opera Liras 1,000 (one thousand)

If for the recording of Discs the Maestro is obliged to leave his residence, he will be entitled to the full amount of his travelling and living expenses whilst away from his abode.

2nd – The Maestro Puccini binds himself not to musically arrange and direct any of his music for any other talking machines for the space of ten years.

The Discs executed under the direction of the Maestro Puccini [are] to have his signature engraved on said discs during the period that this contract is valid.

3rd – The date to be fixed upon for these musical productions will be by mutual agreement.

Perused and approved –
Giacomo Puccini

Milan 2 May 1904

By 4 June 1904, Michaelis also had obtained signed "conducting agreements" with Leoncavallo, Mascagni, Giordano, and Ricitelli. He sent English translations of these agreements to the London office along with translations of contracts for songs to be written by Gustave Charpentier, Henri Rabaud, Francesco Cilèa, Giacomo Orefice, Vincent d'Indy, Georges Pfeiffer, Justin Clerice, Xavier Leroux, and Alfred Bruneau (as well as the contracts for the songs by Puccini, Leoncavallo, Franchetti, Giordano, and Mascagni).[11] As will be seen in the following letters, the London office was not pleased.

B/G   June 10th 1904

Mr. J. B. Vogel
        The Gramophone Company (Italy), Ltd, Milan

Dear Mr. Vogel,

I beg to inform you that Mr. Alfred Michaelis has ceased to represent this Company or The Gramophone Company (Italy) Limited as manager of their Milan branch. Mr. Herbert Douglas Moorhouse holds power of attorney from the Italian Company, and we must ask you to comply only with instructions which you receive from Mr. Moorhouse or from this office.

We request your strict compliance with these instructions, and beg you to acknowledge receipt of this letter by return of post.

Yours very truly,

THE GRAMOPHONE & TYPEWRITER LIMITED
Managing Director

---

11. Other songs published by the Gramophone Company (Italy), Ltd., in 1904 included Henri Rabaud's *Une fée* (text by Gabriel Vicaire); Ch. Silver's *Déclaration* (text by Alexandre Dumas fils); Pfeiffer's *Aimez!* (text by J. Richepin); Mascagni's *Stornelli Marini* (text by Guido Menasci); Cilèa's *Lontananza!* (text by R. Carugati); Leoncavallo's *Ninna Nanna* (text by the composer); d'Indy's *Les yeux de l'aimée*, Op. 58 (text by the composer); and Bruneau's *Chanson de s'amie bien belle* (text by Clément Marot).

B/G   June 10th 1904
H. D. Moorhouse, Esq.
            Milan

Dear Mr. Moorhouse,

At the Board Meeting on Wednesday, it was decided to ask Mr. Michaelis to tender his resignation and, after seeing him, I shall probably wire you to act on your power of attorney. I confirm my wire of last evening: "Expect M. here tomorrow[.] Shall ask for his resignation. On receiving my wire tomorrow take possession under your power instruct Bank re signature. Issue circular to trade announcing resignation recall Vogel etc. confirm receipt. Birnbaum."

It will be necessary for you to take every possible step to prevent Michaelis causing trouble. The first step it will be necessary to take will be to inform the Bank that his signature is no longer valid for the "Manager's" Account, which will be drawn on by you or anyone you may appoint in your stead.

You will also issue a circular to the trade, announcing Mr. Michaelis' resignation as manager of the Milan Company. I should say this as nicely as possible. There is no need to give the slightest explanation; at the same time, there is no need to do anything that would raise comment.

I should like you to report to me what attitude Vogel takes, and if you think he will be loyal to the Company. It is regarded as necessary in London to appoint a manager in Milan ["in the place of," crossed out and replaced by "over"] over Mr. Vogel, as the Board prefers to have someone from the central office whom they thoroughly know, and whom they can entirely rely on.

You will please instruct Secrina to apply for registration of the Company as arranged by me when in Milan.

I have yours of the 6th inst., re rent and taxes. I am astounded to find that our contract runs until 1910. I have no doubt, however, it will be a very easy matter to re-let the premises, should it be found necessary to do so.

Yours very truly,

THE GRAMOPHONE & TYPEWRITER LTD

B/G   June 13th 1904
Alfred Michaelis, Esq.
            The Gramophone Company (Italy) Ltd Milan
Dear Sir,

Confirming our interview of Friday, June 10th., when I communicated to you the decision of the Board, I beg to hand you herewith a copy of the Minute embodying their decision.

The Board decided that the Managing Director "should invite Mr. Michaelis to tender his resignation, failing which, Mr. Michaelis should be deposed from the position of manager of The Gramophone Company (Italy) Ltd."

Yours faithfully,

THE GRAMOPHONE & TYPEWRITER LTD

B/G   June 13th 1904

H. D. Moorhouse Esq.
        Grand Hotel de Milan
        Milan

Dear Mr. Moorhouse,

   We wired you this afternoon as follows: "Please hand Michaelis formal letter
of dismissal confirming my interview of Friday 10th inst., post by registered
letter to his address."

   I have asked you to do this as in the present state of the Minutes of the Italian
Company there is some slight informality in my authority to do so; however,
there can be no question as to your authority to dismiss Michaelis, but it is rather
important that in so doing you should confirm his dismissal as from Friday, the
10th inst.

   Please send me copy of the letter which you write him.

                         Yours truly,

            [THE GRAMOPHONE & TYPEWRITER LTD]

B/G   June 13th 1904

H. D. Moorhouse, Esq. Milan

Dear Mr. Moorhouse,

   I confirm my wire of Saturday. "Michaelis is neither shareholder or [*sic*]
director Italian Company. Have wired Bank authorising your signature."

   For your guidance I think it best to have a copy of the Minutes of the Italian
Company struck off, which I will send you. You will then be able to see what
has transpired since the formation of the Company.

                      Yours very truly,

            THE GRAMOPHONE & TYPEWRITER LTD

B/G   June 15th 1904

Dear Moorhouse,

   I have your telegram [of June 14th] reading: "Michaelis sues me personally
for violent dispossession of premises appear tomorrow no cause for alarm. Can
obtain adjournment. Moorhouse."

   Also your letter of the 13th inst., of which I note contents.

   As to Michaelis' action against you, I do not attach the slightest importance
to this. If it is necessary to give the full grounds of his dismissal I will furnish
you with a statement of them; but you know almost as much about this as I do.

The principal complaints against Michaelis are: that he has closed important contracts without the authority of the Company—for instance, Mascagni, lr. 20,000, etc; that he has not complied with explicit instructions which have been communicated to him from time to time, viz. to discontinue the lawsuit against the Anglo-Italian Company, shipments to Lepage, and so forth. There are also complaints of his service from the Egyptian houses; and many other matters that I could, if necessary, bring into an indictment against him.

You speak of allaying my fears, and that there is no cause for alarm. I beg to say that I am in my normal state of health; and if I have sent you very explicit telegrams and instructions it is more with a view to relieving you of responsibility than anything else. I have come to the conclusion, however, that you are quite able to take care of yourself.

With kind regards,
Yours very truly,

THE GRAMOPHONE & TYPEWRITER LTD

Michaelis' successor, Herbert Douglas Moorhouse, was replaced by Kenneth Muir.[12] Alfred Michaelis subsequently became the managing director of a newly founded rival record company called the Società Italiana di Fonotipia (Michaelis himself had registered the name of this new enterprise in October 1904). In January 1905, he engaged Umberto Giordano to be the musical advisor and artistic director for the Fonotipia Company, and by March of that year they issued their first one-sided records. On behalf of the Fonotipia Company, Michaelis entered into an agreement with Casa Ricordi in May of 1905, thus assuring Fonotipia of access to music from important contemporary operas. Casa Ricordi engraved many of the compositions written specifically for and published by the Fonotipia Company. By 1906, Michaelis had assembled a powerful board of directors that included Harry Vincent Higgins, director of the grand opera syndicate at Covent Garden; Umberto Visconti, Duke of Modrone, then president of La Scala; Tito Ricordi; Francesco Queirazza, a Milanese banker; and the wealthy Baron Frederic d'Erlanger, who also was a noted composer. Michaelis eventually lost the controlling interest in the Fonotipia Company and was reduced in rank to a mere company employee.

In 1907, *Canto d'anime* was recorded by the dramatic soprano Ida Giacomelli for the Gramophone & Typewriter label, and assigned the disc number 53497.[13] Upon a first hearing, the music of *Canto d'anime* reminds one of the patriotic energy of the song "Oh, Columbia, the Gem of the Ocean" and of Rinuccio's civic pride expressed in the aria "Firenze è come un albero fiorito" from *Gianni Schicchi* (1918). In fact, with its dotted rhythms for the voice, the repeated chords in the accompaniment, and the shared B-flat major tonality, *Canto d'anime* could be considered a prototype for Rinuccio's aria. Measures 11–13 are particularly evocative of the musical language of *Madama Butterfly*. Although it was first recorded by a dramatic soprano, with its three top B-flats *Canto d'anime* is well suited to the tenor voice.

---

12. Michaelis' name was printed twice on the cover of the first edition of *Verso l'aurora*, but it was crossed out with a rubber stamp and the name Kenneth Muir was inserted in its place. Moorhouse's name was stamped on the cover of *Canto d'anime*, but it was also crossed out with a rubber stamp and replaced with the name of Kenneth Muir.

13. Raffaele Végeto's discography included in the *Carteggi pucciniani* dates this recording from 1907, and Eugenio Gara's "Prospetto cronologico della vita e delle opere di Giacomo Puccini" (in *L'Approdo Musicale* [Rome, 1959], p. 99) does likewise, but it does not mention a date of composition or publication. Consequently, the prevailing general assumption in the majority of writings about Puccini has been that *Canto d'anime* dates from 1907. Giuseppe Pintorno's chronology and list of Puccini's works published in the house program of *La Bohème* (La Scala, 1976–1977) cites a *romanza* for voice and piano entitled "Canto d'amore" [*sic*], attributed to 1907. It is also rather surprising that Hopkinson's bibliography omits the 1904 publication of *Canto d'anime*.

By 1905, recordings had become an important part of cultural life, and contemporary music was accessible to anyone who owned a phonograph. Record companies were in the process of building major catalogues of operatic scenes and arias performed by leading artists of the day—often without paying any royalties to living composers for the right to record their music. Toward the end of 1905, Puccini was named as the co-plaintiff (with Jules Massenet) in a complicated Belgian lawsuit involving unauthorized recordings, arrangements and transcriptions of their music, as well as the basic question of authors' rights.[14]

During his visit to New York in the winter of 1907 to supervise productions of *Manon Lescaut*, *La Bohème*, *Tosca*, and the revised version of *Madama Butterfly*, Puccini voiced his opinion on the inconsistencies of the American copyright laws in a letter written to the *New York Herald* (and certainly published in the words of a translator) in which he stated:

> During my present visit to the United States I have been repeatedly catechized as to the copyright laws of my own country and requested to compare them with those of America. This I have always declined to do. I am inclined to be rather proud of the fact that my country is among the first in the world to extend to composers the right of controlling the reproduction of their works by means of any and all modern mechanical musical instruments, including the phonograph.
>
> Of course, when our copyright laws were promulgated no such means of reproducing sound waves was dreamed of. Still less than in America, where the modern talking machine was invented.
>
> But Italian courts have held that phonographs are within the copyright law on the broad principle that the originator is entitled to the use and control of his mental creations, regardless of the means whereby they are reproduced for the benefit of the public.
>
> And if the music box manufacturers desire to reproduce my melodies it seems to me that I should have the same liberty of selecting the medium and the method by which they shall be transmitted to the public as I have in choosing the managers and theatres to produce my operas.
>
> Furthermore, while I am heartily glad to note that eminent interpreters of my music, including fellow countrymen like Messrs. Caruso and Scotti, are not only paid princely honorariums for rendering solos from my operas into [*sic*] phonographs, but are also allowed liberal royalties on the sale of those records, it seems strangely inconsistent that the composer of those very themes should not be granted slight pecuniary recognition.
>
> To make the situation still more absurd, these records are so protected by patent that, were I to make a duplicate record of my own compositions, for which I have never granted them any right, these same manufacturers might have cause of legal action against me for infringement in hypothecating the product of my own brain and creative powers.

---

14. See the *Étude critique de l'arrêt de la Cour d'Appel de Bruxelles du 29 décembre 1905 en cause de Jules Massenet et Giacono* [sic] *Puccini contre la Compagnie Générale des Phonographes, Cinematographes et Appareils de Précision et la Société Anonyme C[harles] & J. Ulmann* [sic] by Edmond Picard (Brussels: Veuve Ferdinand Larcier, 1906).

Unlike operatic managers, who produce, and the publishers, who publish a musical work, the manufacturers of these devices exercise no productive effort or stimulate or encourage original work in musical composition, which they exploit for their own gain.

I am sure that the American people, who are firm believers in the principle of justice, equity and square dealing, will join hands with Italy in the suppression of this form of musical piracy.[15]

Puccini's presence in New York was well documented by the American press. On 21 February 1907, one week before their return voyage to Italy, Puccini and his wife, Elvira, participated in a recorded interview with the painter Gianni Viafora for Columbia; however, the resulting disc has yet to be commercially released.[16] *Canto d'anime* remains Puccini's only direct collaboration with the recording industry. (For a report of my findings on the song *Ditele*, believed to have been written by Puccini for the Fonotipia Company, but in actuality composed by a Russian princess, see Appendix II.)

While Puccini was on a holiday in London, he was quoted on the subject again (in an anonymous English translation) in the following "special cablegram" story to the *New York Times* (9 June 1907):

My music has been played and recorded on films and plates, but I have not benefited a sou. Now, if I were to make a copy of one of these films bearing a record of my music, for which, mark you, I have given no permission for transcription, I could be sued for damages. This is rather a humorous view of the injustice of the copyright laws, which I consider very unfair to musicians who have to make a living from the products of their brains. You can hear selections from *Madame Butterfly* and *La Bohème* on these instruments, but I, who composed the works, do not receive a penny from their reproduction.

Along with the memorabilia at the museum of Pucciniana in Celle is a gramophone that was given to Puccini by Thomas Alva Edison himself.[17] According to the composer, "it arrived the very day we installed the electric lights" (see "Puccini lavora" in *Noi e il Mondo*, 1 May 1916). Puccini also kept a signed photograph of Edison in his studio at Torre del Lago. In September 1920, that great inventor sent Puccini a brief note from his laboratory in Orange, New Jersey:

Men die and governments change
but the songs of *La Bohème*
will live forever.
Thos A Edison

Luigi Illica (b. 9 May 1857, Castell'Arquato; d. 16 December 1919, Colombarone) was a self-made poet, journalist, author, and dramatist who began his career writing under the pseudonym of Luigi della Scorziana. Adventurous, volatile, and temperamental (his penchant for dueling and polemics cost him part of his left ear as a result of a confrontation with the director of the *Gazzetta dell'Emilia*), he was also one of the most romantic and witty of the Italian writers

---

15. Portions of this anonymous translation were reprinted in *Musical America*, 9 March 1907, p. 6.

16. A pirated recording exists; a transcript of the session was published in the *Carteggi pucciniani*, p. 372.

17. Puccini, in turn, gave it to his sister Ramelde for Christmas in 1903. The museum, founded by Ramelde's daughter, Albina del Panta, also owns a few of Puccini's records, including marches by John Philip Sousa, salon music for violin and piano, excerpts from an English musical comedy entitled *The Country Girl*, and a few examples of Japanese music—probably some of those Puccini listened to when he composed *Madama Butterfly* (see also Mosco Carner's "The Exotic Element in Puccini" in *Of Men and Music* [London: Joseph Williams, 1944]).

known as the *scapigliati*.[18] Illica's first plays were performed at Milan's Teatro Manzoni; they included *I Narbonnerie La Tour* (1883), written in collaboration with Ferdinando Fontana, librettist of Puccini's *Le Villi* (1884) and *Edgar* (1889); *Il Conte Marcello Bernieri* (1883); *La Signora Leo Pascal* (1884); and *Herick Arpad Tekeli* (1884). From 1886 to 1892, the Teatro Filodrammatici in Milan was the locale for productions of Illica's *Gli ibridi* (1886); *Gli ultimi templari* (1886); *Dramma e melodramma* (written in collaboration with G. Rovetta, 1887); *I diritti dell'amore* (1888); *La sottoprefettura di Roganecca* (1890); *L'Ereditaa del Felis* (written in Milanese dialect, 1892); and *L'anima d'on alter* (also in Milanese dialect, 1892).

Illica is perhaps best remembered as a prolific librettist. In addition to the libretti of Puccini's *La Bohème* (1896), *Tosca* (1900), and *Madama Butterfly* (1904) (all written in collaboration with Giuseppe Giacosa [b. 21 October 1847, Colleretto Parella; d. there, 2 September 1906]),[19] Illica supplied the texts for more than thirty operas, including Catalani's *La Wally* (20 January 1892, La Scala); Franchetti's *Cristoforo Colombo* (6 October 1892, Genoa) and *Germania* (11 March 1902, La Scala); Giordano's *Andrea Chénier* (28 March 1896, La Scala) and *Siberia* (19 December 1903, La Scala), previously rejected as a libretto by Puccini; Mascagni's *Iris* (22 November 1898, Teatro Costanzi, Rome), *Le Maschere* (17 January 1901, with simultaneous premières in six Italian cities), and *Isabeau* (2 June 1911, Buenos Aires); and Montemezzi's *Héllera* (17 March 1909, Turin), also previously rejected as a libretto by Puccini. After the death of Giacosa, Illica made several independent attempts to provide Puccini with suitable libretti (*Maria Antoinetta, Conchita, A Florentine Tragedy*, et al.), but to no avail.

Puccini's forsaking Illica for less experienced, but less argumentative associates proved to be a source of disappointment and irritation to the poet, who had done so much to breathe life into Puccini's three most successful operas. Despite urgings from Puccini and Giulio Ricordi, Illica refused to collaborate with another librettist. At one point in September 1907, he expressed his indignation at the idea in a letter to Puccini. In it he remarked: "If I wanted to be impertinent, I would advise you, and perhaps with greater truth and more justification, that you should take a good musician as a collaborator."[20] Unpredictable and impulsive, Luigi Illica belonged to the last generation of the Risorgimento. He was a man of strong heroic tendencies and deep-felt patriotic zeal. When he was fifty-eight, he volunteered to serve in the Italian army, and from 25 June 1915 through 1916 he was a simple artillery corporal in the 21st Regiment in Piacenza. Ill health, brought on by the hardships he experienced in combat and complicated by arthritis, forced him to leave his beloved regiment. But the day after the disaster at Caporetto, he pleaded with the military officials to allow him to re-enlist: "Comprendo, che alla mia età non sono buono a nulla, ma voglio far qualche cosa di utile per la mia sventurata patria, la vita mi è insopportabile sotto il peso di sì tremenda sventura nazionale." ("I know that at my age I am good for nothing, but I want to do something to serve my unfortunate country. Life is unendurable to me under the weight of such enormous national suffering.")[21] A return to active military service was deemed inadvisable, but the army accepted Illica's magnificent villa in Colombarone for the billeting of certain officers. Illica and his wife, Rachel, also contributed large sums of money to support the efforts of the Red Cross. It was certainly a great joy for Illica to live to see Italy victorious at the conclusion of the first world war. His epitaph is similar to the conviction he expressed in *Canto d'anime*:

Le opere della natura	The works of nature
Sono eterne	Are eternal
La morte non è che una	Death is but a
Nuova vita.	New life.

---

18. See p. 147.

19. Illica also had a hand in the writing of the libretto of *Manon Lescaut* (1893).

20. *Carteggi pucciniani*, Letter No. 524.

21. Quoted by G. E. Ingrao in *La Lettura* (Milan, 1919), p. 950.

CANTO D'ANIME, Pagina d'Album

Fuggon gli anni gli inganni e le chimere
Cadon recisi i fiori e le speranze
In vane e tormentose disianze
Svaniscon le mie brevi primavere.

Ma vive e canta ancora forte e solo
Nelle notti del cuore un ideale
Siccome in alta notte siderale
Inneggia solitario l'usignolo.

Canta, canta ideal tu solo forte
E dalle brume audace eleva il vol lassù,
A sfidar l'oblio l'odio la morte
Dove non son tenèbre e tutto è sol!
Tutto è sol! Tutto è sol!

SONG OF THE SOULS, Album Leaf

The years, the deceptions, and the illusions all flee;
Flowers and hopes are cut down.
In vain and tormented yearnings
My brief springs vanish.

But in the nights of the heart,
An ideal still lives, and still sings loudly and alone
As the solitary nightingale sings forth
In the depth of the starry night.

So sing, sing loudly, my one ideal,
And from the mist, intrepidly soar on high
To defy oblivion, hatred, death
Where there are no shadows, and everything is light!
Everything is light! Everything is light!

CANTO D'ANIME

(Pagina d'album)

Text by
LUIGI ILLICA

Music by
GIACOMO PUCCINI
Edited by Michael Kaye

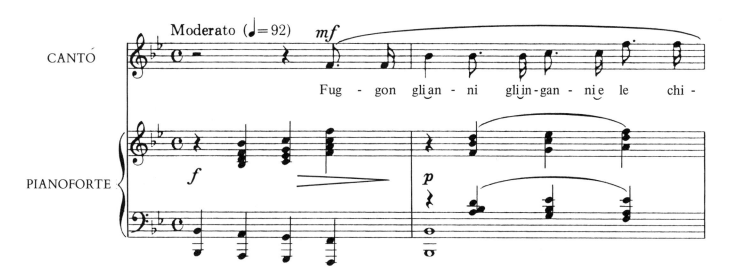

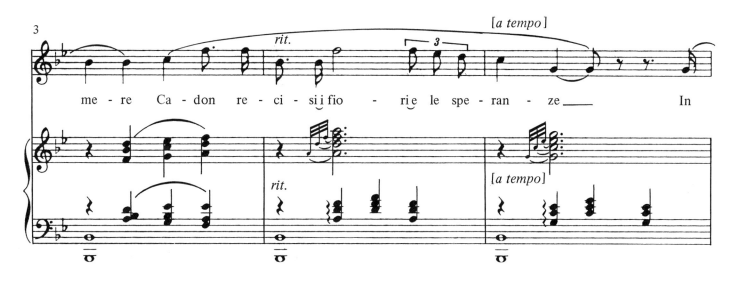

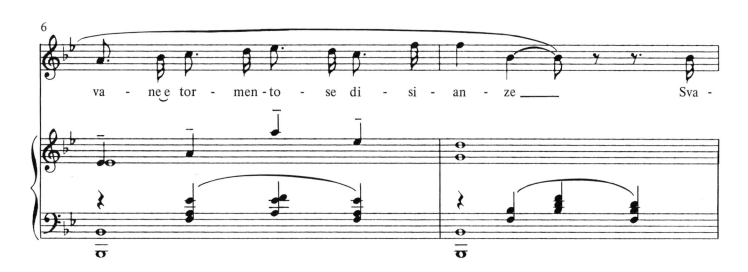

[CASA MIA, CASA MIA]¹

The text, suggested by Edoardo de Fonseca, is a variation on the adage "Be it ever so humble, there's no place like home."

ON 29 NOVEMBER 1908, Puccini completed a questionnaire from his friend Edoardo de Fonseca, the director of the annual album of arts and letters *Novissima*. Six years earlier, Puccini had composed the song entitled *Terra e mare* especially for that successful periodical. The four-page questionnaire in the form of an interview is headed "Le tre case di Giacomo Puccini / Torre del Lago—Chiatri—Abetone." It consists of twenty-three questions in de Fonseca's hand, most of which refer to Torre del Lago, with space provided for Puccini's answers. On the last page, de Fonseca reminds the composer not to forget to send him "una riga di musica: Casa mia, casa mia ecc." ("a line of music [to the words]: Casa mia, casa mia, etc."). Puccini complied with this request. From Torre del Lago, he sent de Fonseca the manuscripts of a brief song, the completed questionnaire, and a signed letter in which he supplied a few more details. These manuscripts are currently in the Dannie and Hettie Heineman Collection in The Pierpont Morgan Library in New York City. De Fonseca published the resulting article together with a facsimile of the musical manuscript in his illustrated fortnightly magazine ("rivista quindicinale illustrata") entitled *La Casa* (Rome: Anno I, Vol. 1, No. 14, 16 December 1908). The text of the manuscript questionnaire reads in part:

Le tre case di Giacomo Puccini
Torre del Lago—Chiatri—Abetone

EF: Torre fu la tua prima casa?

GP: No la 2ª—

EF: In quale anno la comprasti? Come fu, come non fu?

GP: nel [1]900 Era di Don Carlos. Prima abitavo in una casetta in affitto.

EF: Era una casetta, da principio, non è vero?

GP: Era una casa di una guardia di Don Carlos e anticamente era la *Torre* del Lago.

EF: Nella prima casetta quali opere scrivesti?

GP: Nella casa d'affitto parte di *Manon* e *Bohème*.

EF: L'attuale Casa di Torre la edificasti *a fundamentis*?

GP: No era *ti ripeto!* di don Carlos ci scrissi una parte di *Tosca* e tutta *Butterfly*.

EF: Chi fu l'architetto?

GP: diversi—fra i quali io—

EF: Gli ultimi abbellimenti da quando datano?

GP: dall'anno scorso

EF: Dove prendesti i mobili? Furono costruiti espressamente?

GP: da Berardi a Firenze in parte fatti a Torre e a Pisa

---

1. The manuscript is untitled; the square brackets indicate that the title has been assigned based on the first words of the text.

EF: Chi ti fece l'addobbo?

GP: della sala l' [illegible]: Studiati di Pisa

EF: Di qual legno sono i mobili?
1. Dello studio:
2. Della stanza da pranzo invernale:
3. Della stanza da pranzo estiva:

GP: di quercia e [. . .]
GP: di castagno
GP: rustici così detti di vallombrosa

EF: Perchè ami stare a Torre, piuttosto che a Chiatri e all'Abetone? Cioè indipendentemente da ragioni climatiche.

GP: Per la caccia, per la comodità del Treno posta e telegrafo—perchè amo il piano.

EF: Quali ragioni ti spinsero a Chiatri, se tanto amavi Torre?

GP: Comprai Chiatri prima del [1]900 quando ero fuori dell' affitto della 1ª casetta. Fatto Chiatri—mi si offri Torre del Lago—così ebbi 2 case – Chiatri lo comprai per un capriccio.

EF: La villa di Chiatri com'è arredata?

GP: da Berardi e Tedeschi di Firenze

EF: Sintetizza in due o tre parole il paesaggio e i dintorni di Chiatri.

GP: Si vede da Livorno e Spezia l'Arno il Serchio—la Corsica in tempo chiaro le isole [di] Gorgona e Capraia e anche la grande siepe della macchia di San Rossore Migliarino e macchia Lucchese dei Borboni

EF: Perchè salisti all'Abetone ed ora vuoi discenderne?

GP: Salii perchè incantato del sito—voglio scendere per[chè] i 1350 metri mi pesano sto meglio o sul mare o a Chiatri che è a 400.

EF: Dammi un idea dell'Abetone e dei dintorni. Non conosco quel luogo che so bellissimo.

GP: Abeti alti dai 50 a 60 metri Viste splendide clima delizioso strade [illegible] grandi passeggiate per chi ne ha voglia—io non giro a piedi che col fucile—niente caccia. Lassù non si tirano che dei moccoli.

EF: Quali avvenimenti della tua opera d'artista sono connessi ai soggiorni di Chiatri e dell'Abetone?

GP: all'Abetone ho fatto una piccola parte di *Tosca* e *Butterfly*

EF: Nomellini non ha decorato qualcuna delle tue case? Sta sempre a Torre, Plinio?

GP: Nomellini decori la mia sala di Torre ma la tempere si guastò presto e dovetto rifare la sala di nuovo. Plinio non è più a Torre. . . .

EF: Ami la serenità della *home*?

GP: Si— ma è tanto difficile. . . .

EF: Hai da raccontarmi qualche mattacchionata o burla che si riferisce ai tuoi tre soggiorni?

GP: Le ne avrei tante ma ho da lavorare ora son già le 11 di notte e ti saluto. Tuo Puccini. . . .

EF: Domanda ultima: Mi manderai a *casa del diavolo?*

GP: no . . . ma pero se ci penso anche quella li è una casa e tu come direttore ci potresti anche stare – non fosse che nell'inverno così si dice!

The Three Houses of Giacomo Puccini
Torre del Lago—Chiatri—Abetone

EF: Was Torre your first house?

GP: No, the second—

EF: When did you buy it? How did it happen?

GP: In [1]900. It belonged to Don Carlos. Before that I lived in a rented house.

EF: It was a small house at first, wasn't it?

GP: It was the residence of a gamekeeper of Don Carlos and it was formerly the *Tower* of the Lake.

EF: Which operas did you write in the first house?

GP: In the rented house—parts of *Manon* and *Bohème*.

EF: Did you build the present house at Torre *from scratch*?

GP: No, *I repeat*! It belonged to Don Carlos. There I wrote part of *Tosca* and all of *Butterfly*.

EF: Who was the architect?

GP: Several—I among them.

EF: When did you do the latest renovations?

GP: Last year.

EF: Where did you get the furniture? Was it built expressly?

GP: [Part of it by] Berardi in Florence and some of it was made in Torre and in Pisa.

EF: Who did the decoration?

GP: Of the living room [illegible]: Studiati of Pisa.

EF: What type of wood was used for the furniture?
   1. For the study: GP: Oak and [. . .]
   2: For the winter dining room: GP: Chestnut
   3: For the summer dining room: GP: Rustic, Vallombrosa style.

EF: Aside from climatic considerations, why do you enjoy living at Torre rather than at Chiatri or Abetone?

GP: Because of the hunting, the convenience of the train, the mail service and the telegraph—because I love the layout of the house.

EF: Then why did you go to Chiatri if you loved Torre so?

GP: I bought Chiatri before 1900 when I finished renting the first house.

Once Chiatri had been finished Torre del Lago was offered to me. So I had two houses—I bought Chiatri as a whim.

EF: How is the villa at Chiatri decorated?

GP: By Berardi and Tedeschi of Florence.

EF: Synthesize in a few words the landscape and the surroundings of Chiatri.

GP: You can see Livorno and Spezia, the Arno, the Serchio—Corsica. When the weather is clear you can see the islands of Gorgona and Capraia, and also the pine woods of San Rossore Migliarino and the woods of the Borbone family at Lucca.

EF: Why did you go up to Abetone and why do you want to come down now?

GP: I went up because I was enchanted by the place, now I want to come down because the 1,350 meters [altitude] is too much for me. I feel better at sea level or at Chiatri which is 400 [meters above sea level].

EF: Give me an idea of Abetone and environs. I do not know the place which I am told is very beautiful.

GP: Fir trees as tall as 50 or 60 meters. Gorgeous views, delightful climate, roads [illegible], wonderful trails for those who want to walk. I walk around with my gun, but no hunting. Up there you only swear.

EF: Which events of your life as an artist are connected with your stays at Chiatri and Abetone?

GP: At Abetone I did a small part of *Tosca* and *Butterfly*.

EF: Didn't Nomellini decorate one of your houses? Is Plinio still at Torre?[2]

GP: Nomellini decorated the living room at Torre but the tempera decayed very soon and I had to have the room redone. Plinio is no longer at Torre. . . .

EF: Do you love the serenity of *home*? [Here de Fonseca left a large space for Puccini's reply.]

GP: Yes, but it is so difficult. . . .

EF: Can you tell me any silly story or joke related to any of your three houses?

GP: I have many, but now I have to work. It is already 11:00 at night and I am saying good-bye to you. Your Puccini. . . .

---

2. The painter Plinio Nomellini (b. 1866, Livorno; d. 1943, Florence) was one of Puccini's intimate friends. Puccini wrote the following description of his neighbors' reaction to Nomellini's work: "Stasera abbiamo posato l'ovo in casa nuova, acceso tutto...effetto grande straordinario...i tuoi talenti cosparsi sui muri attirano le ammirazioni unamimi di villici e dei cittadini." ("Tonight we have made our nest in the new house, we lit it all up...the effect was extraordinary...your masterpieces on the walls draw the unanimous admiration of villagers and city dwellers.") Quoted by Franco Schlitzer in "Confidenze pucciniane" (*La Scala*, No. 11, June 1959, pp. 40–43).

EF: Last question: will you send me to the devil's den?

GP: No . . . but now that I think of it there, too, is a house and you, as the director, should be able to stay there. Perhaps just in winter as they say!

The questionnaire concluded with de Fonseca's promise to advertise Puccini's house at Abetone for sale in the Christmas issue of *La Casa*. In an autograph signed letter, dated 29 November 1908, Puccini informed de Fonseca that Chiatri was an old villa that originally belonged to the Samminiatis—nobility from Lucca. Puccini refurbished it on an estimate of 30,000 lire, but it ultimately cost him more than 100,000 lire. Abetone was partially completed when Puccini bought it. It was finished under the guidance of his friend Camillo Bardi of Signa. The Florentine architect Castellucci designed the balcony. In an undated postcard to Nomellini, Puccini wrote: "Eccoti il ritratto del nostro villino, ora acquistato. Ti piace? va finito, è tutto in pietra, simpaticissimo." ("Here is the portrait of the cottage we just purchased. Do you like it? It has to be worked on; it is all made of stone, very attractive.")[3]

In addition to being the founding director of *Novissima*, Edoardo de Fonseca was a journalist, art critic, author, and playwright. His works include *Nicolò Barabino,* a study of that Florentine impressionist painter (Florence: G. Scivelli, 1892); *Castelli Romani,* an account of certain towns and villages in Latium, illustrated with original sketches by Roman artists, with an appendix comprising brief descriptions of Tivoli, Anzio, and Nettuno (Florence: Fratelli Alinari, 1904; also published in an English translation by W. G. Cook); a novel entitled *Il Gaudente* (Rome: Novissima, Tip. Unione Ed., 1916); *Old Roman Customs and Traditions Still Surviving: Souvenir of the Palace Hotel* (Naples: Richter & Co., n.d.); and two three-act comedies (*La villa dei lauri* [1922] and *Palma e il suo metodo* [1923]) and a book about Florence (all published in Rome by Novissima, 1927).

At the bottom of the manuscript of the music of [*Casa mia, casa mia*], Puccini added the following postscript: "Caro Edoardo, Io ti consiglio di dare al cestino. Stasera non ero in arteria[4] e tu mi hai forzato a questa altra *cosa* che dichiaro non *mia*. Ciao GP." ("Dear Edoardo, I suggest you use the wastepaper basket. Tonight I wasn't in the mood and you have forced me to this other *thing* that I declare is not *mine*. Good-bye GP.")

---

3. Quoted by Schlitzer in "Confidenze pucciniane," p. 41.
4. The words "in arteria" are a pun on the Italian expression "essere in vena" ("to be in the mood").

[CASA MIA, CASA MIA]

Casa mia, casa mia
Per piccina che tu sia,
Tu mi sembri una Badia,

Casa mia,
Per piccina che tu sia
Tu mi sembri una Badia,
Casa mia, casa mia, casa mia

The text is a variation of the Italian saying "Casa mia, casa mia, benchè piccola tu sia, tu mi pari una badia," an idiom similar to the American sayings "Home sweet home" and "Be it ever so humble, there's no place like home." Literally translated, the text reads:

My home, my home
Though you may be very small,
You seem like an Abbey to me,

My home,
Though you may be very small,
You seem like an Abbey to me.
My home, my home, my home.

[CASA MIA, CASA MIA]

Music by
GIACOMO PUCCINI
Edited by Michael Kaye

1917 [?] MORIRE?

Text by Giuseppe Adami

DURING THE FIRST part of World War I, Puccini felt "stupefied and unable to work."[1] Formerly, he loved to travel to other countries to supervise productions of his operas and reap the benefits of his status as a celebrity composer. On 27 April 1916, he wrote to Sybil Seligman:

> It really is an age since I have given any sign of life! . . . How I long to travel! When will this cursed War be over? It seems to me like a suspension of life. . . . How one longs again for a little life! Here [at Torre del Lago] one languishes; between the green earth and the sea the seeds of hatred against this enforced calm are beginning to develop within me.[2]

While Italy was still a neutral nation, Puccini struggled to maintain an impartial public image. He was not a political person like Gabriele D'Annunzio, Arturo Toscanini, and certain other eminent artists of the day. He was, however, very concerned about the fate of his operas—and the substantial royalties from them in Germany and Austria.[3] Despite his attempts to remain unobtrusively neutral, Puccini became embroiled in a series of controversial international scandals that indicted him as being both pro- and anti-German, a passionate Germanophile, and even a traitor. On 21 December 1914, he wrote to Arthur Wolff, secretary of the German Theatrical Society, in answer to a notice published in *Deutsche Bühne* to the effect that Puccini had joined those protesting German barbarisms against art.

> Dear Mr. Wolff,
>
> I have just heard from my publisher, Mr. Ricordi, that you are counting me among those who have taken a stand against Germany. I am delighted to be able to tell you, on the contrary, that I have ever refrained from any manifestations whatsoever against your country.
>
> Respectfully yours,
> Puccini[4]

The Viennese origins of *La Rondine* later brought accusations in the French press condemning Puccini for unpatriotic acts. Puccini succeeded in extricating himself from these unpleasant imbroglios and subsequently produced tangible evidence of his patriotism. One such example was the song entitled *Morire?*

Morire? was Puccini's contribution to an album of music dedicated to Queen Elena di Savoia and sold to benefit the Italian Red Cross. This album, designated as "Per la Croce Rossa Italiana," was published without any date (but certainly ca. 1917–1918). It also included works by Arrigo Boito, Alberto Franchetti, Umberto Giordano, Ruggero Leoncavallo, Pietro Mascagni, and Riccardo Zandonai. In 1917, the Italian Red Cross had spent more than $3,146,000 for relief work in Italy; by the end of 1918, almost $19,000,000 was required for their efforts to alleviate the enormous suffering wrought by the hostilities. The idea of producing a book to be sold to benefit organizations engaged in relief work was not new. In 1914, Puccini declined an invitation from the British novelist Hall Caine to contribute a composition to "a tribute to the Belgian King and People from representative men and women throughout the world," entitled *King Albert's*

---

1. Later during the war, he managed to compose *La Rondine* and the three one-act operas that comprise the *Trittico*.
2. Quoted in Vincent Seligman, *Puccini among Friends* (New York: Macmillan Company, 1938), p. 265.
3. As a result of Leoncavallo's and Mascagni's public displays of patriotism, their operas had been banned in Germany.
4. Quoted in the 6 February 1915 issue of *Musical America*.

Book.[5] (According to Giuseppe Adami, Puccini considered contributing a funeral march, but he later incorporated that music in Michele's monologue in *Il Tabarro*.)[6] Another notable publication protesting the fate that had befallen Belgium was *The Book of the Homeless (Le livre des sans-foyer)*, edited by Edith Wharton in 1915 and issued simultaneously in the United States and Europe the following year. The proceeds from the sale of that book were for the benefit of the American Hostels for Refugees, the Foyer Franco-Belge, and the Children of Flanders Rescue Committee.[7]

In 1916, Puccini contributed a brief composition for solo piano, marked "Calmo e molto lento," for publication in *Numero Unico* (Turin: Associazione Stampa, November 1916), which was sold to benefit the families of fallen soldiers.[8] Other acts of charity on Puccini's part did not go unobserved. In 1918, he donated an entire year's royalties from performances of *Tosca* at the Opéra-Comique in Paris to a fund for wounded French soldiers. He also authorized a twenty-fifth anniversary production of *Manon Lescaut* at the Teatro Regio in Turin to benefit Italy's Famiglia del Soldato.

Puccini remained in Italy during most of the war. He was able to go to Monte Carlo to attend the première of *La Rondine* at the Théâtre du Casino on 27 March 1917. The profits from this gala event (and from several subsequent performances of the opera) were used to benefit La Protection des Réformés N° 2, a charitable organization of which Prince Albert of Monaco was one of the honorary presidents.

Puccini revised *La Rondine* many times, and it is interesting to note that he used *Morire?* transposed one half tone lower, with a different text and an extended ending for the accompaniment, in the second version of that opera (first performed in Palermo in April 1920 and then in Vienna on 9 October of the same year). In its operatic form, the music of *Morire?* serves as an entrance aria for the tenor Ruggero.[9] This aria was published in Sonzogno's "II Edizione" of *La Rondine* (in Italian only, as "Parigi! è la città dei desideri") and in the Viennese edition of the opera published by Eibenschütz & Berté, entitled *Die Schwalbe* (in German only, as "Paris, ja, das ist die Stadt der kühnsten Wünsche"). Puccini deleted Ruggero's aria from the third version of the score; however, for the purpose of comparison with *Morire?* it is included in the present collection on pages 197–200.

In the context of *La Rondine*, the music of *Morire?* is reminiscent of a romantic aria in the style of Puccini's friend Franz Lehár. In the song *Morire?*, particularly in measures 38–42, one hears the Puccini of *La fanciulla del West* and *Il Tabarro*. *Morire?* is one of Puccini's most unusual compositions, in which occasional ambiguous harmonies underscore the enigmatic nature of Adami's text.

Giuseppe Adami (b. 4 February 1878, Verona; d. 12 October 1946, Milan) studied literature and jurisprudence in Padua. Upon graduating, he became the drama critic for *L'Arena*, a newspaper published in Verona, succeeding Renato Simoni who had accepted a similar position writing for the

---

5. Organized by Hall Caine for *The Daily Telegraph* in conjunction with *The Daily Sketch, The Glasgow Herald,* and the publishers Hodder and Stoughton, 1914, *King Albert's Book* represented a condemnation of Germany's aggression against Belgium. Puccini was not willing to risk the possible boycott of his operas in retaliation and therefore did not participate.

6. Giuseppe Adami, *Puccini* (Milan: Fratelli Treves, 1935).

7. Edith Wharton, ed., *The Book of the Homeless* (New York: Charles Scribner's Sons, 1916). This book included original articles in verse and prose, illustrations, and music by (among others) Léon Bakst, Sarah Bernhardt, Paul Bourget, Paul Claudel, Jean Cocteau, Joseph Conrad, Vincent d'Indy, Eleonora Duse, Charles Dana Gibson, Thomas Hardy, Henry James, Maurice Maeterlinck, Claude Monet, Auguste Rodin, Theodore Roosevelt, George Santayana, and Igor Stravinsky (who contributed the *Souvenir d'une marche boche*).

8. See Magri, *Puccini e le sue rime*, p. 346.

9. "Roger" in the Vienna version. An undated letter written by Puccini to Adami ca. 1915 indicates that Puccini intended to have Ruggero sing a brief *romanza* shortly after he made his initial entrance, but this idea was, at least temporarily, abandoned. The *romanza* did not figure in the first version of *La Rondine* (1917).

Tempo in Milan.[10] Adami also wrote for *La Lettura*, the monthly magazine of Milan's *Corriere della Sera*. He was a successful and prolific playwright of both serious dramas and comedies, including *I fioi de Goldoni* (1905) and *El paese de l'amor* (1907); numerous comedies written in verse and in Venetian dialect; *La sorella lontana* (1908); *La capanna e il tuo cuore* (1913); *Bezzi e basi* (1913; in Venetian dialect), written in conjunction with Puccini's friend and biographer Arnaldo Fraccaroli; *I capelli bianchi* (1915); and at least twenty-five other plays spanning the period 1916–1943. He also wrote many one-act plays, including a trilogy of Harlequin stories for children (*Il vestito d'Arlecchino, Arlecchino mago per forza,* and *Il testamento d'Arlecchino*) for Vittorio Podrecca's famous puppet troupe, I Piccoli di Podrecca, based in Rome.

In 1912, at the suggestion of Giulio Ricordi,[11] Adami attempted to develop a libretto for Puccini entitled *Anima allegra*, based on the Spanish comedy *Genio alegre* by Joaquin and Serafin Quintero. Puccini declined to set it to music[12] but, recognizing that Adami could prove to be a faithful and useful collaborator, he invited him to write the Italian libretto for *La Rondine* (composed in the period 1914–1917 and extensively rewritten from 1918–1922), as well as the libretti for *Il Tabarro* (composed 1915–1916, but not performed until 1918) and *Turandot* (composed 1920–1924; see footnote 10).

Adami wrote many other libretti for operas (including Zandonai's *La via della finestra* [1919]), operettas, and ballets. At various times in his career he wrote and produced Italian-made films (including a version of his 1935 comedy *Felicita Colombo* [1938] and one about Rossini [1943]). After Puccini's death, Adami edited an important collection of the composer's correspondence (*Giacomo Puccini: Epistolario* [1928]) and became one of his biographers (*Il romanzo della vita di Giacomo Puccini* [1932]). Puccini affectionately referred to him as "Adamino."

---

10. From 1920 to 1922 Simoni and Adami collaborated on the libretto of Puccini's last opera, *Turandot* (premièred posthumously in 1926).

11. In 1933, Adami wrote a book about Ricordi, entitled *Giulio Ricordi e i suoi musicisti* (Milan: Fratelli Treves).

12. It was eventually set by Franco Vittadini (1884–1948) to a libretto written by Adami in collaboration with Luigi Motta, and first performed in Rome in 1921.

MORIRE ?

Morire? . . . e chi lo sa qual'è la vita!
Questa che s'apre luminosa e schietta
Ai fascini, agli amori, alle speranze,
O quella che in rinuncie s'è assopita?
È la semplicità timida e queta
Che si tramanda come ammonimento
Come un segreto di virtú segreta
Perchè ognuno raggiunga la sua mèta,
O non piuttosto il vivo balenare
Di sogni nuovi sovra sogni stanchi,
E la pace travolta e l'inesausta fede d'avere per desiderare?
Ecco io non lo so, ma voi che siete all'altra sponda
Sulla riva immensa ove fiorisce il fiore della vita
Son certo lo saprete.

TO DIE?

To die? . . . and who knows what is life!
This one that opens bright and sincere
To temptations, to loves, to hopes,
Or the one that has given up and is drowsing?
Is it the shy and calm simplicity
Which is transmitted like a warning,
Like a secret of hidden virtue
So that each reaches his goal,
Or rather the lively flashing
Of new dreams over tired ones,
And the peace swept away and the inexhaustible belief
  in possessions only to desire more?
Frankly, I don't know the answer, but you who are on the other bank,
On the immense shore where the flower of life blossoms,
I'm certain you will know.

MORIRE?

Text by
GIUSEPPE ADAMI

Music by
GIACOMO PUCCINI

Edited by Michael Kaye

ran - ze, _____ O quel - la che in ri - nun - cie

s'è as - so - pi - ta? _____

È la sem-pli-ci - tà ti-mi-da e que - ta _____ Che si tra-

man - da co-me am-mo-ni - men - to Co-me un se - gre-to di vir-tú se - gre-ta Per-chè o-

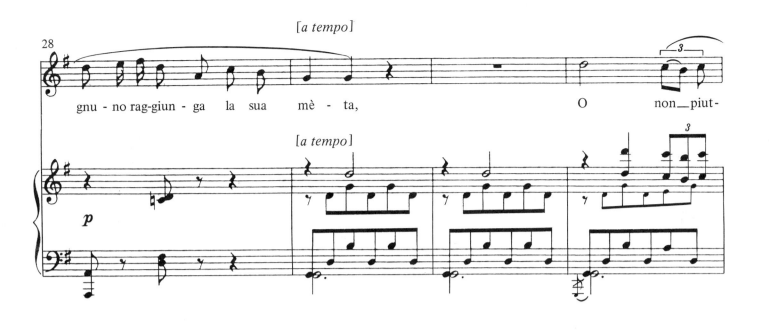

gnu - no rag-giun - ga la sua mè - ta, O non‿piut-

to - sto il vi - vo ba - le - na - re

Di __ so - gni nuo - vi so - vra so - gni stan - chi, E la pa - ce tra -

INNO A ROMA
Text by Fausto Salvatori

This work has often been confused with the *Inno a Diana*, composed in 1897.

IN APRIL OF 1918, the leaders of the city of Rome commissioned Fausto Salvatori, a Roman poet, author, and dramatist who specialized in works of patriotic and religious genres, to write an ode commemorating the Italian victories in what would prove to be the final months of World War I. At that time, Pietro Mascagni was the composer whom the Roman officials intended to invite to set the ode to music so that it could be taught in the elementary schools and sung on solemn occasions. Salvatori graciously accepted the assignment. On 30 May 1918, he submitted the completed text entitled *Alla Madre Immortale* (dated "Il XXII Maggio dell'anno della Guerra Santa di Liberazione MCMXVIII")[1] along with a letter to the Secretary of Public Education, Francesco di Benedetto, in which Salvatori proposed that a competition for composers be held. The winner would have the honor of setting the hymn to music and would receive the prize of an official gold medal. Di Benedetto acknowledged the receipt of the hymn on 3 June, indicating that he would present Salvatori's idea for the competition to the city council. There was a hiatus of several months before contact with the poet was renewed. In the meantime, the war had ended triumphantly for the Allied forces. By January of 1919, the mayor, Prospero di Colonna, and his council had decided to resume the project for a hymn to Rome.

Following the successful European première of the *Trittico* at the Teatro Costanzi in Rome on 11 January 1919, Puccini—Italy's preeminent composer, long a favorite with the House of Savoy[2]—became the logical choice as the person to set the hymn to music. The day after the première of the *Trittico*, Puccini was the guest of honor at a royal reception given at the Villa Ada to celebrate his success, and on 1 February he attended a banquet at the Grand Hotel where he received the title of Grand'Ufficiale della Corona d'Italia. During the toasts made at the banquet Puccini was invited by the mayor to compose the *Inno a Roma*. Puccini returned to Torre del Lago on 3 February; he later received a letter from the mayor, dated 26 February, stating:

> It would be my intention to have [the *Inno a Roma*] sung in the morning by the
> children attending schools on the Palatino: in the evening it could be sung at
> the Teatro Costanzi. I'm writing you this so that you can take it into account
> when you are composing and instrumenting it.[3]

Puccini reluctantly accepted the task against his better judgment. He later came to regret the commitment he had made to the project.

Early in March, Don Prospero wrote to inform the composer that the première of the hymn would occur on 21 April 1919, during the anniversary celebrations for the birth of Rome (*Natale di Roma*). He reminded Puccini that the children would need time to learn the music. Blaming his tardy reply on an attack of influenza, Puccini responded on 16 March:

---

1. The original version of the text is published in Arnaldo Marchetti's "Tutta la verità sull'*Inno a Roma* di Puccini," in *Nuova rivista musicale italiana* (IX, 1975, pp. 397–98), hereinafter referred to as "Marchetti."

2. It should be remembered that Queen Margherita di Savoia provided Puccini with the much-needed stipend that enabled him to attend the Milan Conservatory in 1880. Puccini had dedicated the score of *Madama Butterfly* to Queen Elena di Savoia, and he intended to dedicate *Turandot* to Princess Mafalda.

3. The complete text of this letter is published in Marchetti, p. 400. Unless otherwise stated, the original documents quoted either in whole or in part herein are in the Archivio Capitolino of the Archivio Generale del Comune di Roma, Gabinetto del Sindaco (Anno 1919, fascicolo 70).

Torre del Lago
16 marzo 1919

Carissimo Don Prospero,

. . . Ho letto i versi e ti dico la verità non mi sembrano del tutto adatti, cioè non sono di quel carattere popolare come, a mio avviso, avrebbero dovuto essere. Io mi ci sono provato però—e ti dico la verità—non sono riuscito ad adattarmici. Che fare? Il tempo è corto! . . . Il compito è così grande che mi sento turbato. Ti darò ancora mie notizie. Conservami la tua cara amicizia e non farmi carico se mancassi alla prova.

Affettuosi saluti
Tuo Giacomo Puccini

Torre del Lago
16 March 1919

Very dear Don Prospero,

. . . I have read the [Salvatori] verses and to tell the truth they do not seem to be at all appropriate; that is, they lack that popular character which, in my opinion, they should have had. I have really tried though—and I tell you the truth—I was not able to adapt myself to them. What to do? Time is short! . . . The assignment is so big that I feel upset. I will let you know. Preserve for me your dear friendship and do not hold me responsible if I should not live up to the test.

Affectionate salutations,
Your Giacomo Puccini

On 20 March, Don Prospero wrote:

I am sending you these new verses in which our friend Salvatori has popularized the *Carme Secolare* [by Horace] with a solemn note of Roman flavor.

Three days later Puccini wrote from Torre del Lago:

Carissimo Don Prospero,

Sto impazzendo . . . ma l'inno lo farò! Se non andrà lo cestinerete. Oltre i ragazzi (oh la tirannia della tessitura!) ci vorrà una *ripresa* di popolo e io direi di istruire un certo numero di soldati - Se il canto della 3ª strofa sarà preso a volo come spero, dopo una volta o due, il popolo lo potrà insieme cantare - Fra pochi giorni ho speranza di spedirti la musica - Con affettuosa e antica amicizia,

Tuo G. Puccini

Very dear Don Prospero,

I'm going crazy . . . but I will do the hymn! If it's no good, you can throw it away. In addition to the children (Oh, the tyranny of the tessitura!), it will be desirable to have the refrain sung by the populace, and I would recommend that it be taught to a certain number of soldiers. If, as I hope, the melody of the 3rd stanza will be readily picked up, after having heard it one or two times, the people will be able to sing it in the right place. In a few days I hope to be able to send you the music. With fond and long-standing friendship,

Your G. Puccini

With the preliminary sketches begun, the next day (24 March) Puccini wrote to Maestro Guido Vandini, "I'm crazy to write the *Inno a Roma*," and on 26 March, in a letter to his wife, Elvira (who was in Milan): "I have finished the *Inno a Roma* (a fine piece of rubbish [*una bella porcheria*]), tomorrow Sadun is coming to make the fair copy and I will send it. What will be will be." The manuscript of the *Inno a Roma* (currently in the Museo di Roma) is dated 28 March, not 26 March as Puccini's letter to Elvira would lead one to believe. Puccini asked Icilio Sadun, a young composer of popular songs and operettas who was also copying out some sections of *La Rondine*, to make the presentation copy of the *Inno a Roma* that would be sent to the mayor.[4] At the end of the piece, Puccini had written, "Fine dell'*Inno a Roma* con relativo strapazzo però" ("End of the *Inno a Roma* accompanied by fatigue however"), and then altered the last four words to read "Giacomo Puccini, Torre del Lago, 28 marzo 1919." (On the first page of music he had already written, "G. Puccini, marzo 1919.") According to Marchetti, Sadun received the original manuscript of the *Inno a Roma* as a gift from the composer.

On 2 April, Puccini wrote to Maria Bianca Ginori-Lisci, the daughter of the Marchese Carlo Benedetto Ginori-Lisci:

> Ho scritto l'*Inno a Roma*!!! L'ho spedito a don Prospero ma non so che accoglienza avrà! Sono cose che difficilmente s'imbroccano.
>
> I have written the *Inno a Roma*!!! I have sent it to Don Prospero but I do not know what sort of reception it will have! These things are difficult to guess.[5]

Il Giornale d'Italia of 3 April reported that the hymn had been composed and that Puccini had also sent a copy of the manuscript to Alessandro Vessella, who would score it for his famous concert band. The article quoted from a letter that Puccini had written to Vessella: "È una cosa marziale di pocca [*sic*] entità, penso che possa riuscire di certa popolarità" ("It is a brassy composition of little significance, I think it can achieve a certain popularity"). *Il Giornale d'Italia* also stated that the work would be performed shortly, predicting "an exceptional artistic event." On 10 April 1919, the mayor wrote to Puccini in Torre del Lago:

> Dear Puccini,
>
> I received the music of the *Hymn* and I thank you very much for your kindness and concern. I listened to it played on the piano and liked it very much. I delivered the score and your suggestions to Maestro Vessella, who got to work right away so that it might be possible to have the *Hymn* sung at the Palatino on 21 April on the occasion of Rome's Anniversary.
>
> Cordially,
> Prospero Colonna

On 14 April, *Il Giornale d'Italia* announced that rehearsals had begun, and it published the text of a telegram from the mayor to Puccini:

> Music teachers, public schools present first performance *Inno a Roma* [stop]
> They send through me expressions of admiration and wishes of success worthy of such patriotic significance and [our] illustrious Maestro.—Colonna

The next day the mayor sent Puccini another telegram confirming the première:

---

4. In April of 1919, Sadun's *Il caso di Mimì* was being presented at the Eliseo Theater in Rome.

5. See *Critica pucciniana*, p. 204.

The performance will take place on Monday the 21st [of April] at Villa Umberto at 5:30 P.M. About three thousand performers. Your presence would be greatly appreciated. Best regards.—Prospero Colonna

Puccini, in turn, thanked the mayor and asked him to relay his thanks to the performers and the participating schools. On 16 April, he suggested to the mayor that the text of the poem be published in the newspapers and that copies of the words and the actual music for the refrain of the hymn be printed and distributed to the crowds expected at the première so that they could join in singing, beginning with the words "Sole che sorgi libero e giocondo" (the complete text is given on pages 132–33). On 18 April, the mayor sent Puccini the following specifics:

Dearest Giacomo,

The performers will number about 4,000, including 500 soldiers, the nursery school teachers, the students of the *scuole normali*, the boys and girls of the elementary classes IV-V-VI, the full chorus of the Teatro Costanzi, the municipal band and all the military musicians of Rome, including the brass band of the R. R. Carabinieri, for whom specially made trumpets were ordered for the occasion. This morning at the Teatro Adriano we held the general rehearsal, which turned out marvelously. We have had the program printed with Salvatori's verses for the public and we are sending the civic newspapers the poem and the refrain. We will be happy to have you among us. We have invited all of the authorities, starting with the royal family. In the hope of seeing you in Rome, I clasp your hand fondly.

Very affectionately yours,
Prospero Colonna

At this point in the chronicle, the version of the events as they are described in the Roman press gives more of the story and differs from the data found in Marchetti's monograph "The whole truth about Puccini's *Inno a Roma*."[6] On 20 April, *Il Giornale d'Italia* announced that the site for the première would be the Teatro Costanzi, as part of a gala evening that would include a performance of *Aida*. For the *Inno a Roma*, the chorus of the opera would be supplemented with five hundred soldiers of the Royal Brigade. The newspaper expressed the hope that Puccini would attend.

Marchetti cites two telegrams from Puccini to the mayor on the day before the première.[7] The first one simply stated, "I will come [stop] Express thanks [stop] Affectionate salutations [stop] Puccini"; the second is more obscure: "I'm sorry not to be able to come, I hope everything goes well [stop] please do not repeat [the hymn at the ?] Costanzi because without my instrumentation and without large masses it will not turn out well. Affectionate salutations [stop] Puccini."[8]

The day of the première proved to be a double catastrophe. Puccini need not have worried about the indoor performance in any event, because early that afternoon all of the orchestras servicing the Roman theaters unexpectedly went on strike, forcing the Teatro Costanzi to shut down. The evening gala, as well as an earlier performance of *Madama Butterfly* with Rosina Storchio in the title role, was canceled.[9] By 5:00 P.M., under threatening skies, a huge crowd began to gather

---

6. See footnote 1.

7. I.e., 20 April, not "10 April" as quoted in Marchetti.

8. The fragmented telegraphic style of this message, which literally translated reads "do not repeat Costanzi," makes it difficult to discern Puccini's exact meaning.

9. It was not uncommon for Italian opera companies to give two (and often three) performances in a single day. The first opera usually began at 5:30 P.M. and the second at 9:00 P.M..

in the Piazza di Siena to attend the scholastic festival organized by the Secretary of Public Education, Francesco di Benedetto, on the grounds of the Villa Umberto, and to listen to the concert by Vessella's band along with the performers detailed in the mayor's letter of 18 April.[10] Shortly before 5:30 P.M., some members of the royal family (the prince and princesses, but not the king) arrived in automobiles, to the accompaniment of the *Marcia Reale* (by G. Gabetti)—and so did the first drops of rain! "Without regard for the 5,000 children who were about to raise their silver voices to the sky in praise of the Eternal City, nor for the ladies' finery or the gentlemen's expensive suits" (reported *La Tribuna* of 22 April 1919), bad weather spoiled the event. Just as the first notes of the *Inno a Roma* were heard, heavy rains dispersed the crowd, which was estimated to be in the tens of thousands. The storm persisted and the performance was suspended. *La Tribuna* of 23 April termed the day a disaster. Puccini (who apparently decided to make the trip to Rome after all)[11] was seen backstage at the Teatro Costanzi that evening, while at the box office people were either demanding their money back or, in the case of those who had not already heard about the strike, attempting to purchase tickets for *Madama Butterfly*—whether it was being performed with orchestra or ocarinas.[12]

The *Inno a Roma* première was eventually rescheduled for 1 June 1919, on the occasion of the Royal Gymnastic Competition at the National Stadium, where it was performed at the halftime festivities. Present at the performance were the Prince of Piemonte and the Princesses Jolanda and Mafalda, who had come to see five thousand young gymnasts ("the future soldiers of tomorrow," as they were called in the press) and to hear Vessella conduct his band supplemented by the specially made trumpets of the Carabinieri and a chorus of five thousand young people prepared by Maestro di Miniello. The hymn was greeted with great approbation. That summer, Puccini and Salvatori each received a letter of appreciation and a plain gold watch from the new mayor, Adolfo Apolloni, to mark the occasion.[13]

The *Inno a Roma* was eventually published by the Casa Musicale Sonzogno in 1923. Princess Jolanda di Savoia, who was to be the dedicatee of the Sonzogno edition, became concerned about the future of "her" piece when the firm of Ricordi & Co. declined to publish the work. (According to an agreement that Puccini had signed on 3 December 1916, after a temporary breach with Tito Ricordi, then head of the company, Ricordi had the right of first refusal for any of Puccini's works subsequent to *La Rondine*—the only one of Puccini's stage works Ricordi did not represent. This agreement was operative for as long as Tito Ricordi headed the firm.) On 22 February 1922, Puccini wrote from Viareggio to Maria Bianca Ginori-Lisci:

> Per l'*Inno a Roma* nessuno ne parla più neppure l'editore neppur l'autore. Solo la dolce principessa se ne rammenta! Ed io Le sono molto grato di questo. Scriverò a Sonzogno perchè me ne mandi una bozza—non potè stampare al publico perchè mancavano strofe di poesia—e mai fu domandato al poeta Salvadori [*sic*] di completarle—ma bisogna bene ch'io trovi il modo di servire il desiderio gentile dell'augusta ricordatrice.

---

10. The program (announced in *Il Giornale d'Italia*) was to have been: Overture to Spontini's *Olimpie*, *Norma Fantasy*, *Aida Paraphrase*, the *William Tell* Overture, and the *Inno a Roma*.

11. *Il Giornale d'Italia* of 22 April stated that he had arrived from Venice.

12. The strike, which lasted seven days, forced the Costanzi to close until its spring season began in May, but many other theaters remained open. On 22 April, the Teatro Manzoni presented *Andrea Chénier* with an "orchestra" comprised of three pianos.

13. According to Giuseppe Adami, Puccini had his watch engraved by a jeweler in Lucca; see Adami, *Puccini*, pp. 183–84.

No one any longer speaks about the *Inno a Roma*, not even the publisher or the author. Only the sweet princess recalls it! And I am very grateful to her for this. I will write to Sonzogno so that he can send me a proof—it could not be printed for the public because some verses of the poem were missing—and Salvadori [*sic*] was never asked to complete them—but I really have to find a way to fulfill the kind wishes of the august admirer.[14]

This letter is very curious, for, as we have seen in Prospero di Colonna's letter of 18 April 1919, the text had been sent to the local newspaper. In fact, *La Tribuna* of 20 April published it, preceded by the following notice:

> By kind permission of the poet, we are in the position to offer our readers the complete text of the *Inno a Roma*, by Fausto Salvatori, with music composed by Giacomo Puccini, which will be performed on the 21st of this month at the Teatro Costanzi for the celebration of the birth of Rome.

It is interesting to compare this version of the text with the one published in 1923 by Sonzogno, found on page 135. The version of the *Inno a Roma* published in *La Tribuna* reads:

I

Roma divina, a te sul Campidoglio
Dove eterno verdeggia il sacro alloro,
A te, nostra fortezza e nostro orgoglio,
Ascende il coro.

Salve, Dea Roma! Ti sfavilla in fronte
Il sol che nasce sulla nuova Storia.
Fulgida in arme, all'ultimo orizzonte,
Sta la Vittoria.

Sole che sorgi libero e giocondo
Sul Colle nostro i tuoi cavalli doma:
Tu non vedrai nessuna cosa al mondo
Maggior di ROMA.

II

Per tutto il cielo è un volo di bandiere
E la pace del mondo oggi è latina.
Il tricolore canta sul cantiere,
Su l'officina.

Madre che doni ai popoli la legge
Eterna e pura come il sol che nasce,
Benedici l'aratro antico e il gregge
Folto che pasce.

Sole che sorgi libero e giocondo,
Sul Colle nostro i tuoi cavalli doma:
Tu non vedrai nessuna cosa al mondo
Maggior di ROMA.

---

14. Marchetti's version of this letter (which is quoted from Urbano Barberini's *Strenna dei Romanisti* [Rome: Staderni Ed., 1965]) specifies two missing verses. The translation was made from the letter published in *Critica pucciniana*, pp. 214–15.

III

Benedici il riposo e la fatica
Che si rinnova per virtù d'amore;
La giovinezza florida e l'antica
        Età che muore.

Madre di messi e di lanosi armenti
D'opere schiette e di pensose scuole,
Tornano alle tue case i Reggimenti
        E sorge il sole.

Sole che sorgi libero e giocondo,
Sul Colle nostro i tuoi cavalli doma:
Tu non vedrai nessuna cosa al mondo
        Maggior di ROMA.

The same Sonzogno edition of 1923 also contains another version of the text printed on the page before the music begins. It is entitled "A Roma" and consists of stanzas IA, IB, IC and IIA, IIB, and IIC above. Stanzas IIIB and IIIC were printed in the music, but stanza IIIA was omitted entirely. The probable reason why that stanza could "not be printed for the public" in 1923 was that it would have reinforced an inevitable, but certainly unintended association of the *Inno a Roma* with the *Giovinezza*,[15] which had become the triumphal hymn of the National Fascist Party. Even with the omission of stanza IIIA, Puccini's hymn acquired an unwarranted identification with Mussolini.[16]

When the Casa Musicale Sonzogno published the hymn, the first edition (for voice and piano) bore the dedication "A Sua Altezza Reale la Principessa Jolanda di Savoia." It appeared in March 1923, and on the seventeenth day of that month Puccini was able to write to Maria Bianca Ginori-Lisci: "Dunque le ho spedito l'*Inno a Roma* perchè lo faccia pervenire alla Principessa ormai giu o quasi di grado" ("I have sent you the *Inno a Roma* so that you can transmit it to the Princess [who is] at the present time almost on a lower rank").[17] The first edition was mistakenly titled "Inno di Roma"; however, when Sonzogno reprinted it in 1935 the title reverted to *Inno a Roma*. In 1928, Sonzogno published Vessella's transcription for band, and in 1929 they issued a version for small orchestra by N. Fiorda. In 1930, arrangements were published by Achille Schinelli (for children's chorus) and Silvio Negri (for mandolin orchestra), as well as an anonymous version for mandolin solo. Other arrangements for bands of various sizes were made by Amadeo Amadei (1930) and Michele Mariconda (1936). In 1942, it was published as the *Hymne an Rom*, in an "Instrumentation für grosses Orchester und gemischten Chor von Josef Rixner" (German text by Ralph Maria Siegal) by Ceasar R. Bahar-Edition Baltic, Berlin. Early 78-rpm recordings of the music were made by the baritones Apollo Granforte (1929) and Josef Hermann (in German, 1941), tenor Beniamino Gigli (1937), a children's chorus, the Italian Marine Band, and the Chorus and Orchestra of La Scala, Milan.

In 1935, the *Inno a Roma* was performed before the operas presented at the Baths of Caracalla. The same year, Icilio Sadun sold the manuscript to the Comune di Roma for a reported 25,000 lire.

In addition to writing the text of the *Inno a Roma*, Fausto Salvatori was the author of numerous other works. The majority of these were published in Rome, where Salvatori was born in 1870 and died in 1929.[18] His writings include an untitled collection of poems (1895), another collection entitled *La terra promessa* (1907), and the tragic poem *La furia dormente* (1911). In 1915, several of his pieces (such as *Sonetti libici* and *L'ora Garibaldina*) appeared in the *Rivista di Roma*. That same year, he published a collection of short stories (*Storie di parte nera e storie di parte bianca*) and odes. As a librettist (*Le*

---

15. Music by Giuseppe Blanc, words by Salvator Gotta.

16. After Mussolini's regime, the *Inno a Roma* was remembered by some as the "Inno al Duce," and it is catalogued as such in several American discographies.

17. This probably refers to the princess's impending marriage to Count Calvi di Bergolo, which clearly would be a descent in rank. See *Critica pucciniana*, Letter No. 52, p. 218.

18. Some writers have confused Fausto Salvatori with Giulio Salvadori (b. 1862, Monte San Savino [Arezzo]; d. 1928, Rome), another minor poet of the day.

Eumenidi, music by Filippo Guglielmi, 1905; *La bella e il mostro*, music by Luigi Ferrari-Trecate, 1925; *La fata malerba*, music by Vittorio Gui, 1927) and playwright, he was influenced by D'Annunzio. Salvatori's other patriotic writings include *La canzone dell'ardimento* (1917), *Alla vittoria navale* (1918), and *Genova e Novara* (1918, reprinted in 1922). He also wrote for films and made an adaptation of Shakespeare's *A Midsummer Night's Dream* (*Sogno d'una notte d'estate: Fantasia lirica in tre atti*, 1922).

According to Dante del Fiorentino, Salvatori was mortally afraid of mosquitoes and refused to visit Puccini at Torre del Lago.[19] In 1924, Salvatori wrote the preface to Gino Monaldi's book entitled *Giacomo Puccini e la sua opera*, in which Salvatori said of the composer:

> Giacomo Puccini is a conqueror of multitudes. Even to the heights of the mountains, the rush of the rivers, the oceans, the din of the cities and to countries as yet uncivilized, in theaters made of stone and enriched with gold, and into the tents of the nomadic miners' camps he has brought Italy's flag, the name of Italy, and divine Italian melody like a banner unfurled to the wind in days of victory. It is our duty to honor this most important and best brother of ours; and if one is to honor him one must know him, and more, one must love him.

---

19. See del Fiorentino, *Immortal Bohemian*, pp. 192–193.

INNO A ROMA

I

Roma divina, a te sul Campidoglio
Dove eterno verdeggia il sacro alloro,
A te, nostra fortezza e nostro orgoglio,
        Ascende il coro.

Salve, Dea Roma! Ti sfavilla in fronte
Il sol che nasce sulla nuova storia.
Fulgida in arme all'ultimo orizzonte,
        Sta la Vittoria.

Sole che sorgi libero e giocondo,
Sul Colle nostro i tuoi cavalli doma:
Tu non vedrai nessuna cosa al mondo
        Maggior di Roma.

II

Per tutto il cielo è un volo di bandiere
E la pace del mondo oggi è latina.
Il tricolore canta sul cantiere,
        Su l'officina.

Madre di messi e di lanosi armenti;
D'opere schiette e di pensose scuole,
Tornano alle tue case i Reggimenti
        E sorge il sole.

Sole che sorgi libero e giocondo,
Sul Colle nostro i tuoi cavalli doma:
Tu non vedrai nessuna cosa al mondo
        Maggior di Roma.

HYMN TO ROME

I

Divine Rome, to you from the Capitol
Where the sacred laurel is eternally verdant,
To you, our strength and our pride,
        This chorus ascends.

Hail goddess Rome! On your brow sparkles
The sun that rises on the new age.
Dazzling in arms as far as the eye can see,
        Victory prevails.

Sun that rises free and joyous,
Halt your chariot on our hill:
You will see nothing in the world
        Greater than Rome.

II

Banners are flying throughout the sky
And today the peace of the world is a Latin one.
The Italian flag sings as it ripples over the factory.
        Above the workshop.

Mother of the harvests and of the woolly herds;
Of honest crafts and of thought-filled schools,
The troops return to your homes
        And the sun rises.

Sun that rises free and joyous,
Halt your chariot on our hill:*
You will see nothing in the world
        Greater than Rome.

---

*Literally, "Tame your horses on our hill."

INNO A ROMA

Text by
FAUSTO SALVATORI

Music by
GIACOMO PUCCINI

Edited by Michael Kaye

Ro - ma di - vi - na, a te sul Cam - pi - do - glio Do - ve e -
Per tut-to il cie - lo è un vo - lo di ban-die - re E la

ter - no ver - deg - gia il sa - cro al - lo - ro, _____ A te, no-stra for -
pa - ce del mon-do og-gi è la - ti - na. _____ Il tri - co - lo - re

---

* The 1923 Sonzogno edition states "CANTO DI POPOLO."

tez - za e no - stro or - go - glio, _____ A - scen - de il co - ro.
can - ta sul can - tie - re, _____ Su l'of - fi - ci - na.

Sal - ve, Dea Ro - ma! Ti sfa - vil - la in fron - te Il
Ma - dre di mes - si e di la - no - si ar - men - ti;

sol che na - sce sul - la nuo - va sto - ria. Ful - gi - da in

D'o - pe - re schiet - te e di pen - so - se scuo - le, Tor - na no al -

ar - me al - l'ul - ti - mo o - riz - zon - te, Sta

le tue ca - se i Reg - gi - men - ti E

la Vit - to - ria.

sor - ge il so - le.

dim.

So - le che sor - gi li - be - ro e gio - con - do,

Sul Col - le no - stro i tuoi ca - val - li do - ma:

Tu non ve - dra - i nes - su - na co - sa al mon - do

Mag - gior di Ro - ma, Mag - gior di Ro - ma.

su - na co - sa al mon - do   Mag - gior di Ro - ma,

poco allarg.   *a tempo*

Mag - gior di Ro - ma!

poco allarg.

a tempo

8va - - - - - - - - - - - - *loco*

string.   *rall.*   *a tempo*

PART II

Music Originally Included in Stage Works

LA COPPA È SIMBOL DELLA VITA

Brindisi from the first version of *Edgar*[1]

Libretto by Ferdinando Fontana

THIS VIRTUOSIC *brindisi*, or "drinking song," for soprano (or mezzo-soprano) and chorus was originally sung by the character Tigrana in Act II, scene 2, of the first four-act version of Puccini's second opera, *Edgar* (composed between May 1885 and September 1887). Productions of *Edgar* are rare, but when the opera is revived it more than likely will be heard in the three-act version, which omits this *brindisi*. Puccini finalized this version in February and March of 1905 for a production staged by the Teatro de la Opera in Buenos Aires (8 July 1905). The libretto by Ferdinando Fontana was freely based on Alfred de Musset's armchair drama ("Un spectacle dans un fauteuil") entitled *La coupe et les lèvres* (1832), the title and moral of which stem from the Roman proverb "There's many a slip 'twixt the cup and the lip," or, as de Musset wrote, "Entre la coupe et les lèvres, il reste encore de la place pour un malheur."[2] Puccini received the completed libretto in May 1885. In January of the following year, he wrote from Lucca to Fontana in Milan that he had almost finished Tigrana's aria "La coppa è simbol della vita."[3] The orchestration of *Edgar* occupied Puccini for one year, from 12 September 1886 until the following September when it was completed at Antonio Ghislanzoni's villa in Caprino Bergamasco. The world première of the four-act version eventually took place on Easter Sunday, 21 April 1889, at La Scala, where it was greeted with mixed reactions.

Alessandro Cortella, the critic for *Il Teatro Illustrato*—published by Ricordi's rival Edoardo Sonzogno—devoted ten columns to his review of the première in the May 1889 issue of that magazine. He reported that "the thermometer for measuring its success, which was elevated to a considerable height in the first act, decreased a bit in the second, rose again to enviable heights in the third, where it remained constant for almost the entire fourth act." Puccini was called to the stage three times during the second act, and the *brindisi*, sung by Romilda Pantaleoni,[4] was apparently a "showstopper," admired by Cortella and others for its form, originality, and brilliant vocal effects. Despite its beautiful music, *Edgar* failed to capture the public's fancy (mostly because of the shortcomings of Fontana's preposterous libretto about a vainglorious Flemish youth, Edgar, lured from true love with Fidelia by Tigrana, a gypsy seductress), and the opera was withdrawn after the third performance. At the beginning of 1890, Casa Ricordi published a piano-vocal score of the four-act version in a limited edition of two hundred copies. Puccini dedicated it to J. Burgmein, the pseudonym Giulio Ricordi used to sign his own compositions.[5] Encouraged by Ricordi, Puccini set about revising the opera.

On 5 September 1891, the four-act version was given in Puccini's hometown of Lucca at the Teatro Giglio, where it was a personal and artistic success that culminated in a torchlight procession through the streets amid cheers and further ovations as the audience and populace

---

1. The date 1886 specifically refers to the *brindisi*.

2. This proverb is attributed to Palladas, ca. A.D. 400.

3. Puccini wrote, "Ultimata la Gitana e romanza tenore, e quasi coro e coppa," *Carteggi pucciniani*, Letter No. 22.

4. Pantaleoni (1847–1919), the first Tigrana, had sung Anna at the La Scala première of *Le Villi* (24 January 1885). She was the dedicatee of Ponchielli's *Marion Delorme*, in which she sang the title role (La Scala, 17 March 1885). In 1887, she created the role of Desdemona in Verdi's *Otello*. Verdi had been instrumental in influencing her to accept the part of Tigrana.

5. The following notice appeared in Ricordi's house magazine *Musica e Musicisti* (15 January 1902, p. 25): "Chi è J. Burgmein? Dove, quando è nato? . . . Non lo sappiamo, ed inutilmente abbiamo indirizzato lettere sopra lettere al sig. J. Burgmein: nessuna risposta."

escorted Puccini to his hotel.[6] At a banquet given in his honor following the second performance, Puccini was toasted by Giulio Ricordi as the living hope of Italian musical theater.

Already engaged in the composition of his next opera, *Manon Lescaut*, Puccini made several attempts to revise *Edgar* in the hope of winning lasting audience approval for his much-criticized score. The revisions were extensive. He deleted certain sections, transposed and reordered others. He virtually recomposed and shortened the opera by eliminating the original ending of Act III and replacing it with the final scene of Act IV (the murder of Fidelia by the crazed Tigrana). This condensation of the original four acts to three necessitated the sacrifice of some truly exquisite early Pucciniana.

A slightly abbreviated version of the *brindisi* still figured in the first edition of the three-act version of *Edgar*, published by Ricordi to coincide with the opera's première in Ferrara on 28 February 1892.[7] Puccini made further revisions for a production at the Teatro Real in Madrid on 19 March 1892, but a libretto of the three-act version printed in August of that year still contained the shortened *brindisi*.[8] It appears that Puccini finally decided to eliminate the *brindisi* from the score of *Edgar* when he was preparing the performance version for the 1905 production at the Teatro de la Opera in Buenos Aires.[9] The Sibley Music Library of the Eastman School of Music in Rochester, New York, owns a copy of the 1892 three-act published version of the piano-vocal score containing numerous corrections, modifications, deletions, and annotations in Puccini's hand. This annotated copy corresponds to a later edition (also in three acts) published by Ricordi in April 1905. It is this version that is best known today.[10] In the Eastman score—probably intended as a road map for Carignani and the editors at the Casa Ricordi to use in the preparation of the new orchestra material and piano-vocal scores required for Buenos Aires—the entire *brindisi* is crossed out in blue pencil.

During the course of the revisions, the stage setting for the second act was changed from "in un castello—grande atrio" (in 1890) to a "giardino elegante" (in 1892), and finally to a "perittero d'un sontuoso palazzo" (in 1905). The role of Tigrana (Mona Belcolore in the de Musset play) underwent alterations in tessitura as the opera became shorter. In several instances her music was transposed to lower keys, with much less florid vocal writing and an absence of embellishments and optional high notes that were present in the four-act version. As early as November 1887, Puccini hoped that Tigrana would be sung in Madrid by the Viennese mezzo-soprano Amalia (known in Italy as Amelia) Stahl, who debuted with the Madrid company as Amneris in 1877 and who, for the next twenty years, gained fame in leading mezzo-soprano roles. When *Edgar* finally reached Madrid, Tigrana was sung by Giuseppina Pasqua (b. 19 March 1853 [55?], Perugia; d. 1930, Bologna),

---

6.   In Lucca the opera was sung by Luisa Gilboni (Fidelia), Emma Zilli (Tigrana), Eugenio Durot (Edgar), Cesare Cioni (Frank), and Pio Morini (Gualtiero); the conductor was Vittorio Vanzo.

7.   The Ferrara production was conducted by Carlo Carignani (1857–1919), who had made the piano reduction of the orchestra score of *Edgar*. Throughout Puccini's career, Carignani faithfully served the composer by preparing the piano-vocal scores of Puccini's operas for publication.

8.   The prelude to Act I used in Madrid was a shortened version (108 measures) of the original prelude to Act IV (147 measures) and was not, as is generally thought, additional material composed for that occasion. The signed autograph full score of this prelude, now part of the Robert Owen Lehmann Collection in The Pierpont Morgan Library in New York City, is dated "Madrid / 26 Febbraio / [18]92." Other music originally in the fourth act of *Edgar* was later used in *Tosca*.

9.   The cast of the Buenos Aires production of *Edgar* featured Ada Giachetti (Fidelia), the dramatic soprano Gianinna Russ (Tigrana), Giovanni Zanatello (Edgar), Enrico Nani (Frank), and Remo Ercolani (Gualtiero). The conductor was Leopoldo Mugnone, who led the first *Cavalleria rusticana* (1890), the world première of *Tosca* (14 January 1900), and the La Scala première of *La Bohème*.

10.   Fragmentary souvenirs of the *brindisi* remain in the orchestra part following Frank's "Chi detto a me l'avrebbe mai che della vita mia l'angoscia più crudel saresti stata!" sung in Act I, and in Act III at rehearsal number 35.

who began her career in 1871 as a soprano, singing the role of Oscar in Verdi's *Un ballo in maschera*. (The following year, she sang Amelia in the same opera in Madrid, where, during the 1872–1873 season, she also sang Elvira in *Ernani* and Giulia in Spontini's *La Vestale*.) Pasqua was the first Eboli in the revised four-act version of Verdi's *Don Carlo* (La Scala, 10 January 1884). She continued singing mezzo-soprano roles until the end of her career and is perhaps best remembered as the first Dame Quickly in Verdi's *Falstaff* (La Scala, 9 February 1893).[11] Another member of the world première cast of *Falstaff* sang Tigrana. Emma Zilli (b. 11 November 1864, Udine; d. January 1901, Havana), who created the role of Mrs. Alice Ford in *Falstaff*, sang Tigrana in the successful 1891 Lucca production of *Edgar*. Like her predecessor in the role of Tigrana, Romilda Pantaleoni, Zilli also sang Anna in *Le Villi*. Puccini described her as an "exciting singing-actress," and she became known for her interpretation of his Manon Lescaut. (She also essayed the role of Brünnhilde in *Die Walküre*.) Amadea Santarelli (a Sonzogno artist),[12] the Tigrana of the Ferrara production, began her career as a mezzo-soprano (Amneris in Mexico City, 1894), but later became famous as a *verismo* soprano (Tosca in Santiago, Chile, and the title role in Giordano's *Fedora*). With such a collection of prima donnas it is no wonder that Puccini vacillated between a soprano and a mezzo-soprano version of Tigrana; and, with the onset of the *verismo* movement in Italian opera, a set number with cabaletta-like bolero rhythms and vocal displays such as those found in the *brindisi* was no longer in vogue.

Ferdinando Fontana (b. 30 January 1850, Milan; d. 11 May 1919, Lugano) was a poet, dramatist, journalist, Germanophile, and one of the younger exponents of the bohemian school of writers, artists, and musicians collectively known as the *scapigliati*.[13] He was introduced to Puccini by Ponchielli, who suggested that Fontana write a libretto for Puccini in order to enable the young composer to enter the Sonzogno competition for one-act operas. The resulting collaboration produced Puccini's first opera, *Le Willis*, premièred at the Teatro dal Verme in Milan on 31 May 1884. Fontana was instrumental in raising the funds necessary to mount the Milan première. The title *Le Willis* was subsequently altered to *Le Villi*, and Puccini expanded the opera to two acts for a production at the Teatro Regio in Turin on 26 December 1884. On at least one occasion Fontana acted as an intermediary for the young composer in his early business dealings with Ricordi, and he consciously endeavored to boost Puccini's self-esteem in subtle ways. Puccini had not yet acquired the privileged status he would later achieve as Giulio Ricordi's protégé and the Casa Ricordi's most profitable composer since Verdi.

Fontana attended art exhibitions as an unofficial reporter and published his observations on his own (e.g., *Scalpelli e pennelli: Quarta Esposizione Nazionale di belle arti: rifutati-assenti* [Turin, 1880] and *Pennelli e scalpelli: Esposizione internazionale di belle arti in Roma* [Milan, 1883]). In 1891, at his own expense, he published a collection of his writings in Milanese dialect entitled *Bambann: Bosinad, Sonett, Canzon,*

---

11. The *brindisi* may already have been cut in Madrid, for Pasqua probably found the tessitura uncomfortably high.

12. The two rival music publishers Ricordi and Sonzogno exerted powerful influences on the casting of their operas. At times, both firms were actual presenters of operas in major Italian theaters, representing not only their composers' works, but some of the artists who performed in them as well. In 1895 and 1896, Sonzogno leased La Scala from the boxholders; he was responsible for building the Teatro Lirico in Milan. The firm of Casa Musicale Sonzogno held the exclusive rights in Italy to major works of French composers from the publishing houses of Choudens and Heugel (including *Faust, Carmen, Louise,* operas by Massenet, etc.). Sonzogno would prepackage these operas, along with the Italian operas in his own catalogue, include the scenery, costumes, and artists, and sell the productions to enterprising Italian impresarios.

13. In 1907, Fontana wrote about this "clan" in his article "L'Ortaglia di via Vivajo," published in *La Lettura* (Milan: Anno VII, No. 1, January 1907, pp. 40–48).

Canzonett, ecc. (a set called *Bambann Vecc e noeuv* appeared in 1903). In 1892, he published a pamphlet entitled *Epistola all R. A. Principessa Letizia Bonaparte, Duchessa d'Aosta* (printed in Lecco). His more successful literary works include: *Poeti meneghini* (written in Milanese dialect, 1891); the dramatic poem *Nabucco* (1893); *Viaggi in Europa, in America, in Africa* (1893); *Fra cantanti* (1895); *Giuseppe Grandi: La vita e le opere* (1895); *D'ogni colore: Racconti Arabi, racconti vari* (1898); *In viaggio per la China* (1900); and *Tra gli Arabi* (1912 and 1915). Among Fontana's stage works are the one-act comedy *La statoa del sur incioda* (1890); *La polpetta del re: Lanterna magica per Bagaj F. Bagajoni dai 7 ai 100,000 anni in nientemen che 15 quader per lader et minga, ecc.* (published at his own expense in Lecco [1894], republished as *La polpetta del re: Lanterna magica in quindici quadri* [1908]); and *La leggenda d'Edipo, tragedia in quatro giornate.*

Fontana wrote the libretti for Alberto Franchetti's *Asrael* (1888) and *Il Signor di Pourceaugnac, di G. B. Poquelin de Molière, ridotto ad opera comique in tre atti* (1897); Spiro Samara's *Flora Mirabilis* (1886) and *Lionella* (1891); Vittorio Radeglia's *Colomba* (1887; based on Mérimée); Arturo Buzzi-Peccia's[14] *Forza d'amore* (1897); Angelo Mascheroni's *Mal d'amore* (1898); João Gomes de Araújo's *Maria Petrowna* (1904); Ulisse Trovati's *La Nereide* (1911); and Felice Lattuada's one-act Indian tragedy *Sandha* (published posthumously in 1921). His Italian translations of Franz Lehár's *Die lustige Witwe* (1907) and Eugen d'Albert's *Tiefland* (1910) were performed in Milan and Barcelona, respectively. He also wrote scenarios for ballets, including Riccardo Bonicioli's *Il tempo* (1891) and Romualdo Marenco's *Annibale*. In 1884, Fontana wrote a brief biographical sketch of Puccini for the *Gazzetta Musicale di Milano* (19 October 1884, republished in *Musica d'oggi,* Vol. XV, 1933, p. 148).

Of *Edgar,* Puccini is quoted as having said: "Although I knew that I wrote some pages that do me credit, that is not enough—as an opera it does not exist. The basis of an opera is the subject and its treatment. In setting the libretto of *Edgar,* I have, with all respect to the memory of my friend Fontana, made a blunder. It was more my fault than his."[15] Even though Puccini disowned *Edgar* in his later years, it is obvious from his correspondence and the extensive revisions he made in the score that he hoped this opera would eventually capture the hearts of his international audience. He even considered reusing some part of *Edgar* in his last opera, *Turandot*. In an autograph sketch of the famous aria "In questa reggia," Puccini wrote "assolutamente fatta" ("absolutely done"), then crossed out those words and replaced them with the indication (which he also eventually crossed out) "Forse Aria Edgar" ("Perhaps Aria Edgar").[16]

In a letter written to the publicist Carlo Clausetti six years after the première of *Edgar,* Puccini expressed a certain resentment toward the recognition accorded his earliest operas:

---

14. Buzzi-Peccia (b. Milan, 1856; d. New York, 1943) was one of Puccini's friends from his student days in Milan who became a composer, conductor, operatic coach, and voice teacher. In 1922, Buzzi-Peccia published an abbreviated arrangement of the *brindisi* from *Edgar.*

15. Quoted in Guido Marotti and Ferruccio Pagni, *Giacomo Puccini intimo* (Florence: Vallecchi, 1926). It was always difficult for Puccini to begin composing an opera in earnest until the libretto had reached an advanced state—one that stimulated his musico-dramatic genius, thus enabling him to breathe life into his characters. He was often reluctant to end the process of revising his scores, even after they were established successes.

16. See Karl Gustav Fellerer's article "Von Puccinis Arbeitsweise" in *Die Musik,* Vol. XXX, July 1937, pp. 692–95.

Pescia (Toscana), 9 agosto 1895, venerdì

Caro Carlino,

È inutile, a Milano non mi nominano neppure, non mi chiamano a far parte dei nuovi operisti. Si parla di [Gaetano] Cipollini, di Giordano, di [Spiro] Samara, di Leoncavallo e mai di me! Eppure nessuno di questi (lo posso dire) ha avuto la soddisfazione di farsi applaudire dappertutto in un'opera come me. . . . *Le Villi* hanno iniziato il tipo che oggi si chiama "mascagnano" e nessuno mi ha reso giustizia. Sono in un momento di amarezza!

Pescia (Tuscany), 9 August 1895, Friday

Dear little Carlo,

It is useless, they don't even mention me in Milan; they don't consider me part of the new group of operatic composers. They talk about [Gaetano] Cipollini, about Giordano, [Spiro] Samara, Leoncavallo, but never about me! And yet none of them (if I say so myself) has had the honor of being applauded everywhere the way I was with my opera. . . . *Le Villi* started the trend that today is called "Mascagnano," but nobody has done me justice. I feel very bitter these days![17]

A revival of the original four-act version of *Edgar* might prove interesting. In retrospect, the libretto is no more ludicrous, nor any worse, than many others that are occasionally revived as curios or as vehicles for prominent singers—in fact, it contains several effective scenes. In my opinion, *Edgar* warrants a contemporary appraisal in the opera house.

---

17. Quoted in *Carteggi pucciniani*, Letter No. 127.

BRINDISI[18]

Tigrana, Convitati, Cortigiane, uscendo tulmultuosa-mente dalla sala del banchetto, colle coppe nelle mani, mentre alcuni Valletti sostano in fondo.

CORTIGIANE e CONVITATI
(brandendo le coppe) (ad alcuni Valletti)

Evviva! . . . Le coppe colmate!

TIGRANA
(pure ai Valletti)
A me la mia coppa! . . . Versate!

(I Valletti eseguiscono.)

CORTIGIANE e CONVITATI
Versate, versate da ber!

TIGRANA
La coppa è simbol della vita. . .[19]
Essa all'ebbrezza, al gaudio invita! Ah!
Ecco, la stringe già la man . . .
Ecco, non è il labbro lontan!

CORTIGIANE e CONVITATI
(cozzando i calici)
Godiam! Beviam!

TIGRANA
Ma sta il destino in mezzo a lor;
E forse pria che nel licor
Si bagni il labbro, quella man
Coglie di morte il gelo arcan!
(ridendo)

CORTIGIANE e CONVITATI
La coppa è simbol della vita . . .
Essa all'ebbrezza, al gaudio invita!
Godiam! Beviam!

TIGRANA
Pallida morte, bieca sorte,
Fantasmi orrendi del dolor,
Stringendo in man la coppa d'ôr,
Voi non ci fate più terror!
Pallida morte, fantasmi orrendi,
[Noi vi sfidiam!]
Al varco, o sorte, tu invan ci attendi!
Non ti temiam!

DRINKING SONG[18]

Tigrana, Guests, and Courtiers enter tumultuously from the banquet hall, carrying goblets in their hands. Some Pages waiting in the background.

COURTIERS and GUESTS
(brandishing the goblets and calling some of the Pages)

Hurrah! . . . Fill the cups to the brim!

TIGRANA
(also to the Pages)
Bring me my cup! . . . Pour!

(The Pages do as they are told.)

COURTIERS and GUESTS
Pour! Pour us something to drink!

TIGRANA
The cup is a symbol of life . . . [19]
It invites drunkenness and mirth! Ah!
Look! The hand is already grasping it . . .
See, it is not far from the lips!

COURTIERS and GUESTS
(striking their goblets together)
Let's enjoy! Let's drink!

TIGRANA
But destiny is in the midst of them;
And perhaps even before the liquor
Moistens the lips, that hand is grasping
The mysterious chill of death!
(laughing)

COURTIERS and GUESTS
The cup is a symbol of life . . .
It invites drunkenness and mirth!
Let's enjoy! Let's drink!

TIGRANA
Pale death, malign fate,
Horrendous phantoms of pain,
Golden cup in hand,
We do not fear you any more!
Pale death, fearful phantoms,
[We defy you!]
O fate, you lie in wait for us in vain!
We do not fear you!

---

18. Except where otherwise indicated, the texts of the 1889 and 1892 versions are identical. Puccini did not compose music for the words in square brackets.

19. The published libretto states: "La coppa è immagin della vita" ("The cup is the image of life").

(indicando la coppa)
Per te soltanto l'anima è forte!
Per te la vita ferve nel cuor!
Con te [nel pugno] venga la morte!
D'amor tu additi nei vasti regni
Sogni infiniti! Ah!
Tu sei la magica arte che dà
La voluttà!
Godiam! Beviam!
Vita e coppa fra le dita nell'ebbrezza
Noi stringiam . . . Ah! Ah! Ah!
E afferrando il doppio arcan
Non ha tremiti la man!

CORTIGIANE e CONVITATI
Alle procaci labbra tu insegni
Languori e baci!
Tu sei la magica, tu sei la magica arte che dà
La voluttà!
Della coppa e della vita dunque l'inno
   noi cantiam!
Vita e coppa, vita e coppa fra le dita,
Nell'ebbrezza vita e coppa
Fra le dita stringiam!
(ridendo) Ah! Ah!
Ah! Nell'ebbrezza noi stringiam!
Coppa, risponder tu non puoi!
No! No! Non puoi!
Dell'avvenir che importa a noi?
Dell'avvenir non più chiediam
Se a te libare oggi possiam!
Su via godiam, beviam!
Su via beviam! Ah! Godiam!

TIGRANA
O coppa, O simbol della vita,
[Nell'aria breve . . . ed infinita,
Che il labbro mio sparte da te,]
Dimmi: il destin che serba a me?
[Fors'ei per me creando sta]
Ignote gioie e voluttà,
[Quali nessun quaggiù provò?]
Oppur[20] la morte a me serbò?
Su via godiam, beviam!
Su via beviam! Ah! Godiam!

---

20. "Fors'ei" in the libretto.

(indicating the cup)
Because of you alone the spirit is strong!
Through you, life burns in the heart!
With you [in our grasp] let death come!
With love, you point the way to the vast realms
Of infinite dreams! Ah!
You are the magic art that gives
Pleasure!
Let's revel! Let's drink!
Rapturously we hold tightly
To life and the cup! Ah! Ah! Ah!
And clutching the double mystery
The hand does not tremble!

COURTIERS and GUESTS
To the provocative lips, you teach
Weakness and kisses!
You are the magic, the magic art that gives
Pleasure!
So we sing the hymn of the cup and of life!

Rapturously we hold tightly
To life and the cup!
Life and the cup!
(laughing) Ah! Ah!
Ah! Rapturously, we hold you tightly.
Cup, you can not answer!
No! No! You can not!
What does the future matter to us?
We don't ask about the future any more
As long as we can drink to you today!
Come on! Let's revel! Let's drink!
Come on! Let's drink! Ah! Let's revel!

TIGRANA
O cup, O symbol of life,
[In the short . . . and infinite space,
That separates my lips from yours,]
Tell me: what does destiny have in store for me?
[Is it creating, especially for me,]
Unknown joys and delight,
[Such as no one on earth has ever tried?]
Or am I marked for death?
Come on! Let's revel, let's drink!
Come on! Let's drink! Ah! Let's revel!

EDGAR

Act III, Scene 2

Tigrana's *Brindisi*: "La coppa è simbol della vita"
For Soprano or Mezzo-soprano

Text by
FERDINANDO FONTANA

Music by
GIACOMO PUCCINI

Edited by Michael Kaye

Tigrana - Convitati - Cortigiane

(Uscendo tumultuosamente dalla sala del banchetto, colle coppe nelle mani, mentre alcuni Valletti sostano in fondo.)

153

The second (1892) version states: "Per mezzo soprano si trasporta ½ tono sotto fino al segno 𝄋 " ("For mezzo-soprano transpose ½ tone lower, until the sign 𝄋"). The transposition continued past the *Brindisi*.

154

Poco meno

Pal - li - da mor - te,___ bie - ca___ sor - te, Fan-

tas - mi or-ren - di del do - lor, Strin-gen-do in man la cop-pa d'ôr,_____ Fan-

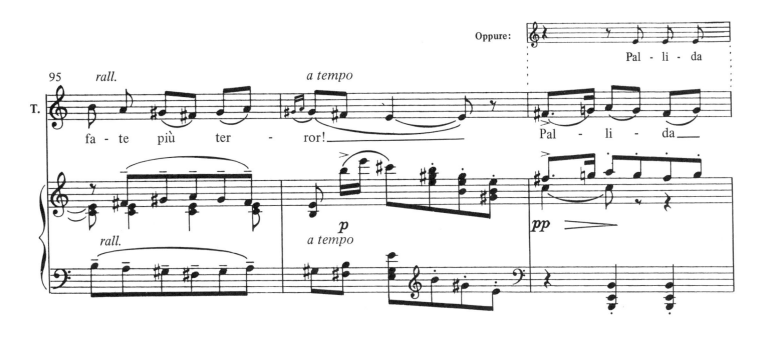

*In the second version (1892), only the lower notes appear.

164

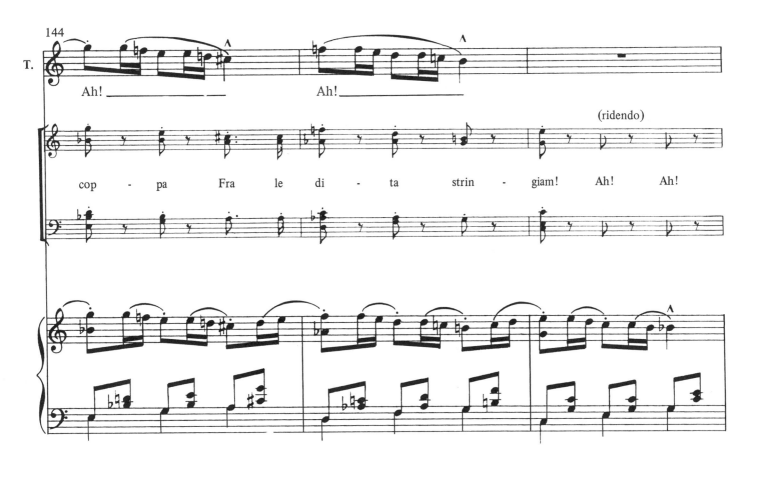

man!
O___ sim - bol del - la vi - - -

giam!___ Cop - pa, ri - spon - der tu non puoi! No!___ No! Non

giam! Cop - pa, ri - spon - der tu non puoi!_____ Non

giam!___ Cop - pa, ri - spon - der tu non puoi! No!___ No! Non

giam!___ Cop-pa, ri - spon - der tu non puoi! No! No! Non

giam!___ Cop-pa, ri - spon - der tu non puoi! No! No! Non

Brillante mosso

---

* In the shorter version. Puccini made the following adjustments in the voice parts:

Brillante mosso

- te! [Tigrana sings in measure 154 as printed on the next page.]

cop - pa__ è sim - bol del - la vi - ta!___

cop - pa è sim - bol del - la vi - ta!

cop - pa__ è sim - bol del - la vi - ta!

cop - pa ___ è - sim - bol del-la vi-ta!___

cop - pa è sim - bol del - la vi - ta!___

* In the second version (1892), Tigrana is tacet in this measure and in the following four measures.

Gilda Dalla Rizza, Puccini, and Tito Schipa rehearsing for *La Rondine*, Monte Carlo, 1917.

Two Excerpts from *La Rondine*

German text by Dr. A. M. Willner and Heinz Reichert
Italian text by Giuseppe Adami

La Rondine has been described as Puccini's most misunderstood work: an unappreciated masterpiece that he alternately called a "porca opera" and "my best music." Its origins are described in the composer's own words in a letter written in April 1917 in rebuttal to Léon Daudet's attacks on Puccini in *L'Action Française* for the unpatriotic act of writing an Austrian opera. The letter was published in the theatrical column of the *Corriere della Sera* of 10 April 1917; it was headed "Le polemiche per la *Rondine* / una lettera di Puccini."

...La mia vita e la mia arte sono i più validi testimoni davanti a tutto il mondo della mia italianità. Ma poichè sono stati esposti al pubblico dei fatti assolutamente inesatti, trovo necessario per puro amore della verità di ristabilirli nella loro esattezza.

Molto tempo prima della guerra io firmai un contratto con una Casa Editrice viennese per un'operetta.[1] I signori Willner e Reichert mi proposero col tramite degli Editori un progetto di libretto che in massima avevo accettato. Ma quando mi accinsi al lavoro, mutai completamente d'avviso. Non mi sentii di scrivere un'operetta e non potevo quindi accettare il progetto di libretto presentatomi. Allora d'accordo con gli Editori e con i librettisti si modificò il primo contratto nel senso che non soltanto lo avrei scritto un'opera lirica e non un'operetta ma che il libretto sarebbe stato scritto da Giuseppe Adami con il quale infatti cominciai a collaborare. Il libretto di *Rondine* nacque quindi da una continua ed assidua collaborazione tra me e l'Adami alla quale i signori Willner e Reichert rimasero estranei. Gli autori del primitivo progetto in questo invertimento esatto di termini sarebbero rimasti quali traduttori in lingua tedesca del libretto di Adami perchè appunto il contratto obbligava la prima rappresentazione di *Rondine* a Vienna e in lingua tedesca.

Aggiungo che nel contratto con gli Editori esteri tanto io che il mio librettista ci eravamo riservati la proprietà assoluta dell'opera nostra

...My life and my art are the most valid witnesses, before the whole world, of my Italianness. But since some absolutely incorrect statements have been made to the public, I find it necessary, for the simple love of the truth, to correct them.

Long before the war, I signed a contract with a Viennese publishing company [Eibenschütz & Berté] for an operetta.[1] Messrs. Willner and Reichert offered me, through the publishers, a suggestion for a libretto which, as a concept, I accepted. But when I set to work, I changed my mind completely. I no longer felt like writing an operetta and I therefore could not accept the proposed libretto as presented to me. Then, in agreement with the publishers and the librettists, the original contract was modified so that not only would I write an opera rather than an operetta, but also that the libretto would be written by Giuseppe Adami, with whom in fact I began to collaborate. Thus, the libretto of *La Rondine* was born of a continuous and assiduous collaboration between Adami and me, to which Messrs. Willner and Reichert remained extraneous. In this exact reversal of terms, the authors of the original project would have [in fact, they did] become the German-language translators of Adami's libretto, because the contract required that *La Rondine* be first performed in Vienna in the German language.

I must add that in the contract with the foreign publishers both my librettist and I

---

1. The original proposal only required Puccini to supply a few separate musical numbers to be interspersed with spoken dialogue. Puccini assigned his author's rights to Eibenschütz & Berté in a document dated 18 April 1914, which confirmed arrangements proposed in a letter of 10 March 1914.

per l'Italia e l'America del Sud. Scoppiata la guerra, assai prima ancora dell'intervento dell'Italia volli sciogliere il mio contratto con gli Editori viennesi onde avere la libera disponibilità dell'opera non soltanto per l'Italia e per l'America del Sud di cui, come dissi, mi ero riservata la proprietà, ma per tutti i paesi del mondo. Essi non mi concessero tale scioglimento ripetutamente e in tutte le forme richieste e allora decisi di non consegnare l'opera già quasi compiuta malgrado ne fossi sollecitato e malgrado per contratto gli Editori dovessero corrispondermi una determinata somma di atto in atto. Tenni dunque la *Rondine* nel cassetto deciso più che mai di trovare la forma di risoluzione del contratto diventato, per lo svolgersi delle vicende politiche, insopportabile al mio sentimento. Un editore italiano intervenne: Lorenzo Sonzogno il quale, sia provocando un decreto ministeriale, sia assumendosi tutte le eventuali cause e responsabilità verso gli Editori esteri, potè offrirmi la completa liberazione della *Rondine,* e quindi, abolendo il primitivo contratto, impegnare con un contratto completamente nuovo me e il mio librettista per la proprietà assoluta dell'opera. Accettai con gioia l'offerta perchè essa coronava la mia volontà e i miei sforzi insistenti.

Quanto all'affermazione che ora a l'Opéra Comique ha rifiutato di far entrare nel suo repertorio la mia ultima opera, devo dire per la verità che nessuna trattativa fu da me e dall'editore iniziata in questo senso. C'è stato invece un impresario che ebbe per conto suo l'idea di portare lo spettacolo [di] Monte Carlo, cioè in lingua italiana, per una sera a Parigi. Quando si chiese la mia adesione (e non erano ancora iniziate le polemiche dell'*Action Française*) io mi opposi recisamente non trovando una rappresentazione episodica nè seria nè utile.

Ecco dunque specificate l'origine e la storia dell'opera mia. E allora l'accusa del sig. Daudet si compendia in questo: io ho sottratto ai nostri nemici quella che era la loro proprietà ed ho ceduta la mia opera ad un editore italiano.

retained the complete rights to the opera for Italy and South America. Once the war broke out, even before Italy's intervention, I wanted to alter my contract with the Viennese publishers in order to have the rights to the opera, not only for Italy and South America, which, as I said, were already mine, but for all countries. [Eibenschütz & Berté] did not grant me this change, which I requested repeatedly and in every possible way, and I then decided not to consign the opera, which was almost completed, in spite of their many requests and in spite of the fact that the publishers were contracted to pay me a certain amount upon the delivery of each act. And so I kept *La Rondine* in a drawer, more than ever determined to find a way to get out of the contract which, because of political events, had become intolerable for me. An Italian publisher, Lorenzo Sonzogno, intervened: by eliciting a ministerial decree and assuming all eventual responsibilities toward the foreign publishers, he could offer me the complete liberation of *La Rondine,* and then having annulled the original contract, he could sign a completely new contract with my librettist and me for the absolute rights to the opera. I joyfully accepted the offer because it crowned my wishes and my insistent efforts with success.

As to the assertion that now the Opéra-Comique has refused to include my latest opera in its repertoire, I must truthfully say that neither [Sonzogno] nor I initiated any such negotiation. Rather, an impresario thought it would be a good idea to bring the entire Monte Carlo production, sung in Italian, to Paris for one evening. When I was asked to support this project (and this was before the polemics in *L'Action Française*) I resolutely opposed it, finding an episodic performance neither serious nor useful.

This then details the origins and the history of my opera. Thus, the accusation of Mr. Daudet comes down to this: I withdrew from our enemies something that was their property, and I gave my opera to an Italian publisher.

Se questo è il mio delitto, ho ragione d'esserne fiero.

La ringrazio e mi dico Suo dev.

GIACOMO PUCCINI

If this is my crime, I have reason to be proud of it.

I thank you and sign myself sincerely,

GIACOMO PUCCINI

The controversial Daudet incident and resulting public rebuttal, which Puccini may have paid the *Corriere della Sera* fifteen thousand lire to publish (see Puccini's letter of 11 November 1919 to Carlo Paladini), troubled the composer for years.[2] His persistent preoccupation with *La Rondine* lasted almost a decade.

Puccini began composing *La Rondine* in 1914. On 21 March 1914, *Musical America* published a report from London, dated 14 March, that stated: "Puccini has signed to write music to *The Swallow*, libretto by Dr. A. M. Willner, author of *The Count of Luxembourg* and *The Dollar Princess*. The work is intended for production in Vienna next winter. . . . Andreas Dippel announced last Tuesday that he had obtained the rights for the United States and Canada to the Puccini-Willner operetta, *The Swallow*, and that he would produce it next year during his season of operetta in New York." On 5 July the *New York Times* announced:

OPERETTA BY PUCCINI

Composed for Dippel, Who Will Give First Performance Here.

Berlin, July 4. An operatic novelty destined to cause a buzz of excitement and interest throughout the international music world will be produced for the first time in New York next season. It is an operetta by Puccini. . . .

He created it specially for Andreas Dippel, under whose auspices the initial performance will be given. Mr. Dippel, who himself suggested the theme, has scored heavily, not only by securing the operetta for America, but by capturing the performing and publishing rights for the rest of the world besides.

Operatic managers, who know the monopolistic practices of the celebrated Italian firm of Ricardi [*sic*], will appreciate the importance of this achievement. Mr. Dippel spent the week in Berlin on a quiet search for new talent. He expects to begin rehearsals for his first season of combined operetta and light opera at some Broadway theatre at the end of August.

His season will hold there until the end of the year, when the Aborn Company relinquishes the Century Theatre for its road season, whereupon the Dippel company will be transferred to Central Park West.

---

2. Léon Daudet (b. 16 November 1867, Paris; d. 1 July 1942, Saint-Rémy-de-Provence) was the son of the famous writer Alphonse Daudet. In March 1917, Daudet and Charles Maurras shared the position of political director of *L'Action Française*, the decade-old Parisian daily "organe du nationalisme intégral" founded by Henri Vaugeois. Daudet was formerly the editor-in-chief of that newspaper. He contended that, in order to secure the première of *La Rondine* for Monte Carlo, Raoul Gunsbourg, director of the Monte Carlo Opera, and Lorenzo (Renzo) Sonzogno must have had dealings with the enemy. In a series of caustic articles published from January through May 1917, Daudet repeatedly accused Gunsbourg and Sonzogno of espionage and treason. He asserted that, in secret meetings held in Switzerland, Gunsbourg and Sonzogno had consorted with the Austrians for the purpose of acquiring a large number of Viennese operettas along with some German operas, which (according to Daudet) they "intended to produce in Italy, France, England and America under the names of young unknown Italian composers and as works of famous old masters." Daudet also indicted Adami, demanding that Adami certify that the libretto of *La Rondine* was entirely his own. (See also footnote 32.)

The Dippel episode in the history of *La Rondine* has been a lacuna in published biographies of Puccini and in writings about the opera. Dippel (b. 30 November 1866, Kassel; d. 12 May 1932, Hollywood) was a former singer—one of Mahler's favorite tenors in Vienna—and an artistic manager, second in command to Gatti-Casazza at the Metropolitan Opera, and later to Cleofonte Campanini in Chicago. In May 1913, Dippel resigned under pressure from the Chicago Grand Opera Association, but he was paid twenty-five thousand dollars, an amount equal to his next year's salary, with the proviso that he not reenter the operatic field as a private impresario for three years. This left him completely open for operetta. Dippel succeeded in producing a limited but popular series of lavishly mounted operettas (*The Lilac Domino,* 44th Street Theater, 28 October 1914, etc.) with prominent singers in New York City and on tour. It is true that he pursued Puccini, demanding a work to fulfill his vision of "grand operetta" for the masses; however, he failed miserably in his first solo venture as an opera producer when his Interstate Opera Company floundered in Pittsburgh (late December 1916).

In the spring of 1914, Puccini wrote to his Viennese friend Angelo Eisner von Eisenhof:

> Lasciali dire i nemici. Anche qui si dice che mi sono abbassato a far l'operetta come Leoncavallo!! Questo mai e poi mai. Poi, come lui, non mi riuscirebbe neppure a farlo apposta.

> Let the enemies talk. Here, too, they say that I lowered myself to write operettas like Leoncavallo!! This will never happen. And then, just like him, I couldn't do it, even if I tried.[3]

On Christmas Day 1914, Puccini wrote from Milan to Eisner in Vienna:

> *Rondine* è a buon punto, due atti son compiuti. Dimmi, dato lo stato delle cose attuali spaventose per l'orribile guerra, cosa succederà di questa opera?

> *Rondine* is in good shape, two acts are finished. Tell me, what do you think will happen to this opera now that things are in such a frightful state because of this horrible war?[4]

Italy declared war on Austria-Hungary on 23 May 1915; Eibenschütz, Berté, and company were automatically enemies of Italy. The Italian press was filled with anti-Viennese sentiments, some of which were directed at Puccini's friend Franz Lehár:

> Ed i walzer per cui Vienna è famosa?
> E l'operetta a Vienna come va?
> E il sublime Franz Lear [*sic*] che cosa fa?
> E la vedova allegra non si sposa?

> E le dame viennesi dalla posa
> languida e piena di sensualità
> dal violino espertissimo che sa
> il lamento che l'anima riposa?

---

3. *Carteggi pucciniani,* Letter No. 646. According to the original contract for *La Rondine,* Eisner von Eisenhof was to receive 7 percent of the royalties collected by Eibenschütz & Berté and 3 percent of Willner and Reichert's royalties.

4. Ibid., Letter No. 665.

Franz Lear compone per i reggimenti
marcie funebri a fascio e gli tzigani
mangiano le minugia agli strumenti.

E le dame viennesi, donne strambe,
suonano ritirate a quattro mani,
e il guerrier si ritira a quattro gambe.[5]

The first version of *La Rondine* was finalized by Easter of 1916, and on 17 November of that year Puccini described the situation in a letter to Sybil Seligman:

> This War which goes dragging on and silences every thought which is not connected with it, generates in me that state of inertia which I already possess in great measure. I am at war with my publishers; I have two operas ready and nothing has been decided—one of them has no money and the other (that's Tito) occupies himself with other matters than music—all the same he telegraphed to me yesterday and it seems that he will agree to my terms for the *Tabarro*. . . . I am going to give one opera at Monte Carlo—I don't know whether it's going to be the *Rondine* or *Tabarro*. It will be in March.[6]

A SURVEY OF THE PUBLISHED EDITIONS

La Rondine is the only one of Puccini's stage works that is not published by Ricordi & Co. The history of its publication is a tangled affair. Tito Ricordi, who succeeded his father as the director of the firm, did not believe in the *Rondine* project from the start. He disliked dealing with Eibenschütz and Berté, and they were unable to come to terms concerning proprietary control of the opera and the editorial rights for its international representation. Early on, Ricordi was too involved in the shaping of the libretto of Riccardo Zandonai's *Francesca da Rimini* (first performed in Turin, 19 February 1914) to be burdened with the Viennese originators of *La Rondine*. Puccini found Tito's behavior degrading. They quarreled, and events led to a brief personal breach between them. In the beginning of September 1915, Puccini met with Emil Berté in Interlaken, Switzerland, and secured permission from the firm of Eibenschütz & Berté to arrange for a première of the opera outside of Vienna.

On 31 July 1916, Puccini informed Ricordi that he had received proposals from Sonzogno and that *La Rondine* could not be kept on the shelf any longer. Puccini was clearly upset by the prospect of dealing with another publisher after so many years of loyalty and success with Casa Ricordi. By 19 September 1916, Puccini knew that the Casa Musicale Sonzogno, Ricordi's strongest rival, would represent the opera—at least in Italy. Contrary to what Puccini stated in the *Corriere della Sera,* Sonzogno was not able to completely liberate *La Rondine* from the clutches of the Viennese. The facts are that in 1920 Eibenschütz & Berté represented and published the opera in Vienna; and since 1928 the rights to the opera have been shared by Sonzogno and the famous Viennese publishing house of

---

5. One of the "Sonetti Viennesi" published in *Numero Settimanale-Umoristico-Illustrato* (Turin, 20 June 1915, Anno III, No. 78); in English it reads: "And the waltzes for which Vienna is famous? And how is operetta in Vienna doing? And what is the sublime Franz Lehár up to? Isn't the merry widow going to get married? And what about the Viennese ladies with those sensuous languid poses to the very skilled violin that knows the lamentation that lies within the soul? Franz Lehár composes funeral marches for the regiments by the score and the tziganes eat the guts out of the instruments. And the Viennese ladies, whimsical ladies, beat out retreats with their hands, and the soldier retreats on all fours."

6. Vincent Seligman, *Puccini among Friends,* pp. 266–67.

Universal Edition.[7]

Around the time that Puccini signed his contract with Sonzogno he settled his differences with Tito Ricordi—at least for business purposes. They reaffirmed their relationship in a letter of agreement granting Ricordi & Co. the right of first refusal for all of Puccini's works subsequent to *La Rondine.*

La Rondine was published in three different versions in Puccini's lifetime. The first version (1917, reengraved in 1929) represents the work as it was originally, and is now, performed. The second version comprises changes that were executed in productions mounted in Palermo (Sonzogno's "II Edizione," 1920) and Vienna (1920). The third, and most extensively revised version (Sonzogno's "III Edizione," prepared ca. 1921–1922), has never been performed. Giuseppe Adami's name does not appear anywhere in the score of the Vienna version (Eibenschütz & Berte: plate number E & B 231), and the names of Willner and Reichert are omitted from the first edition of 1917. The German libretto of the Vienna version is of particular interest, for it is the work of the creators of the scenario, Dr. Alfred Maria Willner and Heinz Reichert (not, as is usually stated, that of R. St. Hoffmann).[8] As a result of the shared ownership of the rights to *La Rondine,* Sonzogno represents the work in Italy and its colonies, England and its colonies, and in France, French Switzerland, Spain, Portugal, Monte Carlo, South America, Egypt, and Tunisia; Universal Edition claims the opera in the rest of the world. I am very grateful to the Casa Musicale Sonzogno and to Universal Edition for their cooperation and permissions to publish the excerpts from *La Rondine* in this collection.

THE FIRST VERSION

Puccini remained in Italy for most of the war, but he was able to travel to Monte Carlo for the première of *La Rondine* at the Théâtre du Casino on 27 March 1917. This gala event was given to benefit La Protection des Réformés N° 2, an organization that aided invalid soldiers. Following the favorable review of the première in *Le Matin* of 1 April 1917 was a brief declaration signed by Puccini that reads:

> J'ai écrit *La Rondine* en 1912 [*sic*] sur un livret italien du poète italien Giuseppe Adami. Cette oeuvre devait être crée à Vienne. J'ai rompu le contrat. J'ai retiré ma pièce spontanément et je la donne gracieusement à l'Opéra de Monte-Carlo, au bénéfice de l'oeuvre française de protection des réformés n° 2 et des blessés italiens.

---

7. Many important documents pertaining to the original Sonzogno contracts were lost during World War I and when Sonzogno's Milan offices and archives were destroyed by bombing in August 1943. According to documentation provided by Universal Edition, they did not represent Eibenschütz & Berté prior to 1921. On 17 August 1924, Puccini wrote to Riccardo Schnabl: "Ora a Vienna ci sarà la causa per liberare *Rondine* dagli editori austriaci" ("Now in Vienna there will be a lawsuit to liberate *Rondine* from the Austrian publishers"). (Simonetta Puccini, ed., *Giacomo Puccini: lettere a Riccardo Schnabl* [Milan: Emme Edizioni, 1983], Letter No. 135.) The firm of Eibenschütz & Berté was bought by Universal Edition in 1927. On 5 November of that year, *La Rondine* was given in Kiel in a production billed as an "Umarbeitung der Operette zur Oper." The *Jahrbuch* of Universal Edition announced: "Im Jahre 1928 . . . Abmachungen mit dem Hause Sonzogno über die Oper *La Rondine*" (*Universal [Gesang] Jarhbuch,* 1929, pp. 121–22). It may surprise some readers to know that in 1929 Kirsten Flagstad sang the role of Magda, in Swedish, in Göteborg.

8. In 1929, a later edition of the first version was issued jointly by Eibenschütz & Berté (in name only), Universal Edition, and Casa Musicale Sonzogno. It includes Adami's Italian text and a "New German verwon [*sic*]," and lists the librettists as "Dr. A. M. Willner, Heinz Reichert / Giuseppe Adami." Its German text is cited as a "Rückübertragung aus den Italienischen von R. St. Hoffmann." This is the only version of the score still commercially available (bearing the combined plate number UE 9653 E & B 231). When it was reprinted in 1969 for sale in the United States, the "re-translation" by R. St. Hoffmann was replaced by an English version by Robert Hess.

According to provisions of the Berne Copyright Conventions, the Monte Carlo Opera had the anomalous privilege of presenting productions of artistic and literary works without their authors' consent—providing that proceeds from these performances were utilized for charitable purposes (see the *Gaulois du Dimanche* of 1–2 February 1913).

"The première of *La Rondine* was a real surprise," wrote the critic Jules Méry in *Le Figaro* of 30 March 1917:

> Although he remained himself, Mr. Puccini revealed himself in a new light. Never before had this great charmer expressed such a delicate lightness and a fine gaiety without abandoning his expressive force. *La Rondine* is a true comedy full of sentiment and full of charm.[9]
>
> The main action revolves around Magda's love for Ruggero. She is a fashionable Parisian during the Second Empire, and he is a young student. Magda, who flies toward love as a swallow flies toward sunny places, leaves her rich protector and her luxurious life to realize her dream to love and be loved. Ruggero, who ignores Magda's past, wants to marry her. She refuses. Her conscience awakens her from her dream, and she sacrifices herself. The pardon would not erase the past.
>
> Mr. Puccini's music is better than a shower of melodies. It is an uninterrupted melody. Whether the dialogue is a sung conversation or a series of long expressive sentences, whether the chorus participates in the action or the orchestra alone comments on a situation, the melodic flow is inexhaustible—underlined by an orchestration that is full of marvelous touches.
>
> Since the first night, *The Swallow* seems to have established its destiny to fly around the world. Mr. Puccini, who attended the première, sat in the royal box of His Supreme Highness, the Prince of Monaco [Albert I]. At the end of the first act, Puccini was acclaimed by the public and obliged to take a bow. With the mounting success after each scene, the audience called for the composer after the second act, and again after the final scene.
>
> The management of the Monte Carlo theater produced the work with truly artistic care. The lyrical couple of Magda and Ruggero found two admirable performers in Miss [Gilda] Dalla Rizza and Mr. [Tito] Schipa.[10] Miss Dalla Rizza is a young and beautiful singer with a magnificent voice, and Mr. Schipa is a young tenor with a splendid voice and a vibrant sense of comedy. The comical couple of Lisette and Prunier was remarkably interpreted by the lovely and subtly mischievous Miss [Ines Maria] Ferraris, and the tenor, Mr. [Francesco] Dominici, a perfect singer and an elegantly comical comedian. Mr. [Gustave] Huberdeau added his usual qualities of subtlety and authority to the beautiful vocal quartet. . . .

---

9. Puccini described *La Rondine* as a *commedia lirica*. Aside from the obvious parallel with certain works by Franz Lehár, the choice of the descriptor *commedia lirica* was probably influenced by the *Komödie für Musik* descriptor that Strauss attached to *Der Rosenkavalier*, an opera Puccini admired.

10. Puccini originally wanted Rosa Raisa and Giulio Crimi for the roles of Magda and Ruggero, but they were both singing in Chicago at the time. Even though Monte Carlo was an oasis of peace during World War I, neither Raisa nor Crimi wanted to risk the journey to Europe. See also Letter No. 28 in Simonetta Puccini's *Giacomo Puccini: lettere a Riccardo Schnabl* in which Puccini confidentially expresses some doubts about the choice of Dalla Rizza: "D'altronde chi prendere? La Raisa è rimasta in America e non ha torto." Despite this temporary concern on Puccini's part, Gilda Dalla Rizza was one of his favorite artists. Rosa Raisa, of course, created the role of Turandot; Crimi created the roles of Luigi and Rinuccio in the *Trittico*.

Mr. Visconti's decors are living proof of that master's talent. As to the orchestra's performance under the direction of the young Maestro [Gino] Marinuzzi, it was admirable for its suppleness and its coloring. This young Italian is a great conductor.

Claude Trevor, the critic for *The Musical Standard,* termed the première "the musical event of the present season on the Continent." Earlier on the day of the première, Puccini was appointed a Grand Officer of the Order of Saint Charles at a ceremony held aboard the royal yacht, which appropriately enough was named the *Hirondelle.*[11] Twelve days later (on 8 April), he wrote to his cousin Vittorina Balestrero, who insisted on having all of the scores of Puccini's operas, "Non è ancora uscito lo spartito della *Rondine*; a suo tempo te lo manderò" ("The score of *La Rondine* has not yet been published; in due time I will send it to you").[12]

"PROBLEMS AND PAINS"

The first version of *La Rondine* was subsequently performed in Buenos Aires (24 May 1917), Bologna (2 June 1917), Rio de Janeiro (1 September 1917), and Milan (Teatro dal Verme, 7 October 1917). It was in Milan that Puccini's difficulties with *La Rondine* in the theater began. The cast of the Milanese production included Maria Farneti (Magda), Toti dal Monte (Lisette), Gennaro Barra (Ruggero), and Francesco Dominici (Prunier), conducted by Leopoldo Mugnone. On 4 October 1917, Puccini wrote to his friend and librettist Giovacchino Forzano:[13]

> Sono guai e dolori! Stasera doveva essere la generale. Non sarà e può darsi che io faccia una solenne protesta. Tenore cane, donna incognita per ora. Buona al piano, sulla scena incognita, ripeto perchè il *mancio* [Mugnone] è quanto ci può essere di più grossier! La commedia sparisce. Io lo dicevo prima, ma sono stato ingannato e poi attorniato perchè cedessi. Renzo è scomparso, c'è Arnoldi e stasera, dopo la prova del fuoco, o scoppia la bomba o viceversa. Situazione sfibrante, vorrei esser lontano mille miglia!

> Nothing but problems and pains! Tonight should have been the dress rehearsal; however, it will not take place and I might make a formal protest. The tenor [Barra] is a dog, the woman [Farneti] is unknown for the time being. She's good at the piano rehearsals but is nothing distinguished on the stage . . . the *left-handed* Mugnone embodies everything that is grotesque. The comedy disappears. I had said this before and I repeat it now, but I was tricked and talked into doing this. Renzo [Sonzogno] has disappeared, Arnoldi is here and tonight, after the ordeal by fire, either a bomb will explode or vice versa. It's a debilitating situation, and I would like to be a thousand miles away![14]

---

11. The presentation ceremony, held on 27 March 1917, was reported in the *Journal de Monaco* of 3 April 1917. The latter date has been mistakenly cited in some sources as the date of the ceremony.

12. Quoted in "Puccini e il 'mal della pietra'" by Pietro Berri (*La Scala*, No. 128, July 1960, pp. 16–19).

13. Forzano (b. 19 November 1883, Borgo San Lorenzo; d. 18 October 1970, Rome) was the librettist of *Gianni Schicchi* and *Suor Angelica*, two one-act operas that, with *Il Tabarro*, comprise Puccini's *Trittico*. Puccini also consulted with Forzano for suggestions to improve the libretti of *La Rondine* and *Turandot.*

14. Arnaldo Marchetti, *Puccini com'era* (Milan: Edizioni Curci, 1974), Letter No. 445.

The day after the production opened, Puccini wrote to Forzano again:

> I giornali dicono di tutto un po' di *Rondine*. Io non li ho letti. Solo il *Corriere* è
> buono, ma di tutto questo io non mi preoccupo nè mi attristo molto. Quello
> che a me angustia è vedere l'opera mia così male interpretata! Quel Mugnone
> è veramente deleterio: nessuna *finesse*, nessuna *nuance*, nessuna *souplesse*, 3 cose
> così necessarie in *Rondine*. Grosso il 1° atto; confuso, squilibrato e scolorito il
> 2°; grosso il 3° in principio e vaccamente enfatico nel resto. Insomma fra *donna*
> (e non mi sbagliavo nell'a priori giudicarla), tenore squadrato e scorretto senza
> un'ombra di bel canto e *Lui*, sono stato massacrato. L'uditorio fu anche troppo
> buono per l'opera.
>
> Renzo non s'è visto. Se ci fosse stato gli avrei fatto capire che con questi
> criteri la *Rondine* non va trattata. Sarà sempre un dispiacere continuo, se non si
> provvede a delle interpretazioni adatte all'opera.

> The newspapers say a little bit of everything about *Rondine*. I haven't read
> them. Only the *Corriere* [*della Sera*] is good, but I am not really worried about
> this, nor does it make me very sad. What distresses me is to see my opera so
> badly interpreted! That Mugnone is really harmful; no *finesse*, no *nuance*, no
> *souplesse*, three things that are so necessary in *Rondine*.[15] The first act is rough;
> the second is confused, unbalanced and colorless; the beginning of the third is
> also rough, and the rest of the act is so grossly emphasized that it totally lacks
> grace. In short, between the *woman* (and I was not wrong in my previous
> opinion of her), the tenor (squarish, rude and inaccurate, without a shade of
> bel canto) and *Him* [Mugnone], I have been slaughtered. The audience was
> even too kind toward the opera.
>
> Renzo didn't show up. If he had been there I would have made him
> understand that *Rondine* cannot be treated in this fashion. It will always be a
> continuous disappointment if appropriate interpretations are not provided for
> the opera.[16]

In January 1918, *La Rondine* was given at the Teatro Costanzi in Rome—with Dalla Rizza,
Gigli, Nerina Marmora, and Dominici, conducted by Ettore Panizza—where, in Puccini's words,
"it went well." The next month it was presented in Naples (26 February), but the opera was failing
to achieve the widespread popularity of Puccini's previous works. Furthermore, during and
immediately following the first world war, major international opera companies were hesitant to
stage what they considered an Austrian-inspired controversial concoction with connotations of
operetta. Puccini was unhappy about his business relationship with Sonzogno, who was not pleased
with Puccini's penchant for making extensive revisions long after one of his operas had been
engraved and published.[17] On 29 June 1918, Puccini confided his displeasure with the situation in a
letter to Sybil, who he hoped would somehow be able to secure a London première of *La Rondine*:

> I find myself at loggerheads with my Italian publishers, and I should not be
> indisposed to enter into negotiations with some English publisher. . . . I am

---

15. Leopoldo Mugnone (1858–1941) was a conductor whom Puccini formerly held in high regard.

16. Marchetti, *Puccini com'era*, Letter No. 447.

17. Many of Puccini's "final" thoughts on his music, his orchestrations, and the staging of his operas are not in the
published scores. As late as August 1922, he was revising *Manon Lescaut* for a production at La Scala to be conducted by
Toscanini.

not bound in any way to *Savoia*[18] except for the right of pre-emption, which means a sort of preference which would automatically disappear in face of a *strong* English bid with which he certainly couldn't compete. But I don't want to write direct to Boosey or to any other publisher.

For the *Rondine* I received 250,000 lire—do you think it would be possible on this basis to come to an arrangement? It would be a question of the rights all over the world.

I warn you that in addition to this premium there are the percentages for royalties, etc., and a percentage on the publication of the music, which would be a matter for discussion and on which we could come to an agreement. If you know of anyone you could trust and who could enter into negotiations, write to me. . . .

How happy I should be to come to an arrangement with an English publisher and to be able to get out of the clutches of these publishers of ours![19]

THE SECOND VERSION

During the summer of 1918 Puccini set about formally revising *La Rondine* for potential productions in Florence, Naples, Palermo, and Rome. According to Giuseppe Adami, who repeatedly obliged the composer by modifying the libretto, "Puccini was always convinced that *The Swallow*, one day or another, would resume her flight . . . he loved to linger over the sparkling music with a kind of tenderness for this child of his which had not succeeded, like the others, in filling the theaters of Italy and the rest of the world."[20] On 5 July 1918, Puccini wrote to Renzo Sonzogno:

> Mi occorre l'intera partitura di *Rondine*. Ho fatto dei preziosi accomodi e piccoli validi cambiamenti al primo atto: Prunier baritono, Lisette rialzata di tessitura, Rambaldo più evidente, Ruggero meno stupido, e Magda finisce il primo atto cantando con efficacia. [See musical example.]
> Per il secondo vedremo il da farsi. Intanto converrà cambiare la *mise en scène*, cioè lo scenario. Per il terzo son dolori! È un gran scoglio, perchè il soggetto è il grande nemico. Aspetto Adami di giorno in giorno; con Forzano abbiamo lavorato, ma per il terzo ci troviamo a disagio; ma le ripeto: vedremo. Intanto mi mandi la partitura, così preparo le correzioni per acquistar tempo.

I need the full score of *Rondine*. I have made some very valuable alterations and small valid changes in the first act: Prunier [is now a] baritone,[21] Lisette is raised in tessitura, Rambaldo more evident, Ruggero less stupid, and Magda ends the first act singing with effectiveness. [See musical example.]

For the second act, we'll see what must be done. At least it would be better to change the *mise en scène*, that is, the scenario. For the third act there are problems! It's a great obstacle, because the plot is the great enemy. I am waiting for Adami day after day;[22] I have worked with Forzano, but we do not feel comfortable with our ideas for the third act; but I repeat: we shall see. In the meantime, send me the score, so I can prepare the corrections to gain time.[23]

---

18. "Savoia" and "the Czar" were some of Puccini's nicknames for the dictatorial Tito Ricordi, whom Puccini considered "a queer, capricious fellow."

19. Seligman, *Puccini among Friends*, pp. 278–79. The Puccini-Seligman correspondence indicates that there was some interest from an unnamed British publisher, but nothing came of it.

20. Giuseppe Adami, ed., *Giacomo Puccini: Epistolario* (Milan: Mondadori, 1928), p. 118. According to a letter to Sonzogno of 16 July 1918, neither Puccini nor Adami requested any compensation for the changes they made in the score that year.

21. In the first version Prunier had been a tenor; in the third version this reverted to a tenor role.

22. Adami was then in the army.

23. *Carteggi pucciniani*, Letter No. 721.

The final measures of Act I in the second version:

Ines Maria Ferrari, Puccini, and Gilda Dalla Rizza in Monte Carlo, 1917. Courtesy Casa Musicale Sonzogno.

Ten days later Puccini wrote to Sonzogno:

> È qui Adami, abbiamo aggiustato primo e secondo, o meglio ci siamo intesi. Quando ritornerà fra 10 o 12 giorni colle idee del terzo sarebbe bene che ci fosse anche lei. Io vorrei cambiare *mise en scène* secondo e terzo, e sarei anche del parere di lasciar da parte l'odiosa crinoline e rimettere l'opera in veste moderna stilizzata tipo Brunelleschi. E se questo signore lei lo potesse rintracciare e portarlo qui alla seduta fra circa 10 o 12 giorni?

> Adami is here; we have adjusted the first and second acts, or rather, we are in agreement. When he returns in about ten to twelve days with the ideas for the third act it would be good if you could be here as well. I would like to change the *mise en scène* of the second and third acts, and I would also be of the opinion to forget about those hideous crinolines and reset the opera in modern dress in the style of Brunelleschi.[24] Could you get in touch with him and bring him here to the meeting in about ten to twelve days?[25]

On 8 August 1918, he informed Sonzogno:

> La romanza al primo atto per il tenore è pronta, come pure sono pronti tutti gli arrangiamenti, cambiamenti e accomodi del primo atto, e non son pocchi, vedrà.

> The *romanza* for the tenor in the first act is ready, as are also all of the adjustments, changes and alterations for the first act, and there are quite a few, you will see.[26]

In a postscript to an undated letter to Adami, Puccini expressed his desire to include a "little *romanza*" for Ruggero to sing in Act I:

> Al 1° atto lascerei l'equivoco e metterei la romanzetta tenore al punto dove Rambaldo gli domanda: "è la prima volta che venite a Parigi?" Qui la romanzetta e per conseguenza l'affare delle mani sia corto.

> In the first act I should leave out the scene of the mistake and put the tenor's *romanzetta* at the point where Rambaldo asks him: "è la prima volta che venite a Parigi?" The *romanzetta* here, and then, as a result, let [the palm reading scene] be short.[27]

Puccini evidently changed his mind, for there is no *romanza* (or even a *romanzetta*) for Ruggero in the first version of the opera; nor does one figure in the third version. In the second version, it occurs shortly after Ruggero (Roger as he is called in German) enters. Puccini also used this music, transposed to G major with variations in the accompaniment and a different text by Adami, as the song for voice

---

24. When Umberto Brunelleschi, a well-known Tuscan painter and costume designer, proved to be unavailable for the assignment, Puccini proposed to engage the equally famous Luigi Sapelli (better known as Caramba). Both of these artists provided designs for the première of *Turandot*.

25. *Carteggi pucciniani*, Letter No. 722.

26. Ibid., Letter No. 726.

27. Adami, *Epistolario*, Letter No. 127. The position of this undated leter in Adami's collection indicates that it was written in late 1915 or early 1916, although it may actually date from 1918. Notwithstanding, other changes Puccini requested in this letter, i.e., the trio for Lisette, Prunier, and Magda in Act III, are realized in the second version (see footnote 29).

and piano entitled *Morire?* (included in this collection on pages 123–26). Was this music originally conceived for *La Rondine*, or was it first composed as Puccini and Adami's contribution to the album of music sold to benefit the Italian Red Cross? At this juncture it is impossible to give an unequivocal answer.

In August of 1919, Puccini was in touch with friends in Vienna. Carlo Paladini helped him contact Franz Lehár and Julius Korngold, the famous music critic for the *Neue freie Presse*. On 31 August 1919, Puccini wrote to Paladini: "Ora sono al rifacimento di *Rondine* e mi secca tanto! Speriamo che non sia minestra riscaldata" ("Now I am working on remaking *Rondine* and I am very tired of doing it! Let's hope that it will not be like warmed-up soup").[28] The previous day he had written this letter to Renzo Sonzogno:

> Adami ha rifatto la *Rondine* e mi pare bene; anche il terzo atto avrà altra soluzione che sarà logica e soddisfacente; ora mi metto al lavoro e appena pronto, atto per atto, lo manderò allo stabilimento per l'incisione, così ci troveremo l'edizione pronta più presto.
> Prego lei di voler rifondere le spese del viaggio ad Adami.

> Adami has redone *Rondine* and I think well; the third act too will have a different solution that will be logical and satisfactory; now I will get to work and as soon as I have each act ready I will send it on to the office for engraving so that we will get the publication ready sooner.
> Please send Adami a reimbursement for his travel expenses.[29]

The polemics of the past still haunted him. From Torre del Lago, on 7 November 1919, Puccini sent the following important letter to Carlo Paladini:

> Ho ricevuto giorni fa un giornale da monaco baviera nel quale si dice tra l'altro (a proposito di una ripresa di *Bohème*) che i maestri tedeschi prendessero esempio da quella musica che va nel cuore e che la loro è troppo cerebrale e finiva con un inno alla melodia! e questo in Germania! Ieri sera venne da me Renzo Sonzogno reduce da *Vienna* – cosa disse della mia musica *là* non so' dirlo senza arrossire – della ripresa di *Bohème* all'ex imperial teatro, coi prezzi della première di Strauss, un teatro da far paura e entusiasmo – e concluse che era fiero d'essere italiano, per me – e che da per tutto era onorato e riverito perchè disse che era l'editore di Puccini. Scrivo questo, lo sai perchè - non certo per farmi l'autoreclame – ma . . . siccome sento voci dall'altra parte e dalla mia niente – è per reazione – Mai un corrispondente da Berlino o da Vienna o da Parigi (dove 3 volte per settimana mi si eseguisce) ha mai scritto una parola.
> Ciao, scusa lo sfogo.

---

28. Paladini, *Giacomo Puccini,* p. 118.

29. *Carteggi pucciniani,* Letter No. 761. The solution to the third act probably refers to the alteration of the denouement: Ruggero gives Magda a ring, after which Prunier and Lisette enter and attempt to influence Magda to return to Paris. Magda resists, confident of her love for Ruggero. Prunier finally persuades Magda that she must leave Ruggero. The opera ends with Magda, brokenhearted, removing Ruggero's ring and, supported by Prunier, walking off in the distance.

A few days ago I received a newspaper from Munich in which it was said, among other things (regarding a new production of *Bohème*), that German composers should use as models for their music the music that goes straight to the heart, and that their music is too cerebral, and the article ended with a great praise for melody! And this in Germany! Last night Renzo Sonzogno came to see me. He has just come back from *Vienna*. What he said about my music over *there* I can not tell you without blushing. He told me about the revival of *Bohème* at the former imperial theater, about the prices for the Strauss première—a theater to awe and enrapture[30]—and he ended by saying that I made him proud to be Italian and that whenever he said that he was Puccini's publisher he was honored and revered. Do you know why I am writing you this? Certainly not to glorify myself, but . . . I hear there is a lot of talking about the other part [his controversial public image], but nothing about me, so this is a reaction of mine. No correspondent from Berlin or Vienna or Paris (where my music is played at least three times per week) has ever written a word about me.

Ciao, excuse my outburst.[31]

On 11 and 12 November 1919, Puccini sent Paladini the following letters. The first, written in the evening, probably refers to Puccini's rebuttal to Léon Daudet (see above); it reads in part:

> contratto di Vienna? Ferri? – bei porci - sul disfattismo non dico niente - se mai ci fu, fu per me e non coram populo come faceva il chiacchierone del mio collega - per dirtene una diedi 15,000 lire sonanti al *Corriere*. Il contratto di Vienna fu fatto il 1913! come potevo prevedere?

> Vienna's contract? Ferri? - they are pigs - I'm not speaking about the defeatism - if there ever was any it was for me privately and not publicly as my bigmouth colleague made it seem - and to tell you something more, I gave 15,000 lire in cash to the *Corriere* [*della Sera*]. The Vienna contract was done in 1913! How could I have foreseen?"[32]

---

30. Puccini was probably referring to the world première of *Die Frau ohne Schatten* (Staatsoper, Vienna, 10 October 1919). Sonzogno was the Italian agent for Adolph Fürstner and thus represented Richard Strauss' operas in Italy.

31. Paladini, *Giacomo Puccini*, Letter No. 9.

32. Paladini, *Giacomo Puccini*, Letter No. 10. Guido Ferri was a photojournalist who, along with the writer Arturo Lancellotti, had interviewed Puccini at Torre del Lago for the magazine *Noi e il Mondo*. The resulting article, entitled "Puccini lavora," was published on 1 May 1916. In it Puccini responded to questions about *La Rondine*:

— È un opera leggera. E mi fate già abbastanza noie.
— Prima di essere rappresentata?
— Prima, sì. Un disgraziato contratto mi lega ad un' impresa viennese. Ho fatto di tutto per rescinderlo, dichiarandomi pronto a rinunciare alle 250,000 corone convenute, ma senza nulla ottenere. Per l'Italia la proprietà è mia; per l'estero no. E dovrò sopportare che la prima rappresentazione si dia a Vienna.
— Quando?

The next day he continued in the same vein. In this second letter to Paladini, Puccini refers to his letter of 21 December 1914 to Arthur Wolff, secretary of the German Theatrical Society. The text of that letter may be found on page 119.

> Io per l'accusa di disfattismo ho il mio papiro (?) la lettera scritta ai tedeschi al tempo in cui tutti principiando dal Re eravamo neutralisti – fu un passo falso lo so – ma non fui io – fu Tito Ricordi che mi chiamò da qui a milano e *volle* per gli interessi della casa (più che per i miei) redarre la lettera, che mi valse noie parecchie specie in Francia - ma tutto fu accomodato da Tittoni ed io rilasciai i diritti d'autore per la *Tosca* ai feriti francesi.

> Concerning the accusation of defeatism I have [found] my [old] papyrus, the letter written to the Germans at the time when all of us, starting with the King [on down], were neutralists. It was a mistake, I know, but it wasn't I, it was Tito Ricordi who called me from here to Milan, and wanted, in the interests of *his* firm (more than my interests) to prepare the letter for publication [probably in the *Corriere della Sera*] that gave me so much trouble—especially in France—but everything was worked out by Tittoni, and I released the rights for *Tosca* to the wounded French.[33]

In April 1920, Puccini wrote to Riccardo Schnabl: "E *La Rondine* ti piacque? . . . A Palermo con Gui pare andata bene nella nuova Edizione" ("And did you like *La Rondine* [referring to the revival at Monte Carlo on 22 March 1920]? . . . In Palermo with Gui it seems to have gone well in the new edition").[34] Puccini wrote this letter ten days after the opera had been staged at the Teatro Massimo in Palermo, on 10 April 1920. Linda Cannetti sang Magda, a role she had already performed during the 1917-1918 season in Bergamo; Thea Vitulli was the Lisette; Ettore Cesa-Bianchi, a dramatic tenor who sang in *Lohengrin* and *La Walkiria* at La Scala, was the Ruggero; Rambaldo was sung by Umberto di Lelio, a first-class buffo of much renown (and the father of Mrs. Franco Corelli); and Vittorio Gui conducted. Most significantly, in Palermo the role of Prunier was sung by the dramatic baritone Cesare Formichi, an artist of excellent fame at Covent Garden and in Chicago. It is probable that the Sonzogno "II Edizione" was used for the Palermo production; however, Puccini made further revisions for the Vienna version.

— Dopo la guerra, si capisce. Ma è antipatico lo stesso. D'altronde siamo innanzi a una questione legale complicatissima. Se manco al contratto sono certo di venir chiamato innanzi ai tribunali austriaci che potrebbero condannarmi pure a un milione di danni. E non sarebbe una condanna platonica, perchè a poco a poco finirebbero col prenderselo, sequestrandomi i diritti d'autore.

Posta la questione così, non c'è nulla da opporre. Un milione per la guerra non l'ha messo ancora fuori nessun privato, per quanto forte possa essere lo spirito di patriottismo italiano. - Del resto - egli aggiunge - da un pezzo di percentuali non ne veggo più ombra dagli Imperi Centrali. Le mie opere continuano a tenere il cartellone a Vienna e a Berlino e i conti non arrivano.

— E . . . il boicottaggio francese?

— Ma sono frasi. In Francia, in Inghilterra la *Bohème*, la *Manon*, la *Butterfly* si rappresentano continuamente.

By quoting portions of this interview in his own context in *L'Action Française*, Léon Daudet implied that Puccini was guilty of commercing with the enemy. At a private luncheon party that Puccini attended in 1919, Guido Ferri had evidently criticized Puccini for being a defeatist.

33. Paladini, *Giacomo Puccini*, Letter No. 11. Tommasso Tittoni was the Italian ambassador to Paris from 1909 to 1915, and subsequently represented his country in other capacities. See also Mario Simonatti's article entitled "Où M. Puccini rentre en scène," published in *Union latine* (Paris, 25 February 1917), in which Simonatti mentions Puccini's letter to Wolff, discusses Tittoni, and accuses Renzo Sonzogno of having dealings with the Austrians.

34. Simonetta Puccini, *Giacomo Puccini: lettere a Riccardo Schnabl*, Letter No. 51, dated 20 April 1920.

During the summer of 1920, Puccini learned that in the autumn the Vienna Staatsoper would present the Austrian première of the *Trittico*. By September, the Vienna Volksoper announced its intention to mount the long-delayed Viennese première of *La Rondine*. Puccini made plans to arrive in Vienna for rehearsals on 23 September, but these plans had to be changed. He thought that his friend Felix Weingartner would conduct; however, Weingartner, who had left the Volksoper in the lurch, was guest conducting in America. The assignment fell to a *Kapellmeister*, Pietro (Peter) Stermich (di Valcrociata). The première was originally set for 1 October 1920 but was rescheduled for 7 October. The *Neue freie Presse* of 5 October reported that Puccini (and his wife) arrived in Vienna from Lake Como that morning and "went from the train station, where he was met by friends, to the new Hotel Bristol. He used the morning to take walks and make visits. Tomorrow he will be attending the dress rehearsal of his work ["seines Werkes"] *La Rondine* at the Volksoper." The theatrical column of the *Neue freie Presse* of 6 October documents that Puccini began work the day he arrived.

At the morning rehearsal (on 5 October) he was introduced to the artists by Karl Lustig-Prean, the acting intendant who was also staging the première. That evening Puccini himself led an ensemble rehearsal and announced that he wanted to make some small changes in the final hours that remained before the dress rehearsal. Stermich translated for the composer as he addressed the company. Puccini had "unusually complimentary things to say about the artists' accomplishments." The *Neue freie Presse* added: "In conversations with friends and admirers today, Puccini stressed again his warm feelings for Vienna and expressed his sincere sympathy for the serious troubles that we are currently contending with. He repeatedly spoke of the beautiful Vienna of the past, about the splendid days of the *Bohème* première. Without reproach for the temporary publicity trend directed against him, Puccini can confidently assert that he has remained a warm friend of the German people."

Apparently Puccini was not all that satisfied with the state of affairs at the Volksoper. On the day of the première, the *Arbeiter-Zeitung* announced:

> Because Giacomo Puccini has decided to make musical changes in his opera *La Rondine*, [35] the première will not take place tonight, but rather on Saturday [9 October]. In its place, there will be an open dress rehearsal.

---

35. In the Viennese press, *La Rondine* was frequently referred to by its Italian title rather than as *Die Schwalbe*, the published title of the Vienna version.

On 8 October 1920, an in-depth article by Josef Reitler headed "Puccini's *La Rondine*—First Performance at the Volksoper" (obviously written well in advance of the première) appeared in the *Neue freie Presse*:

Seven years ago, while he was spending several weeks in Vienna on the occasion of the first Viennese performance of his opera *The Girl of the Golden West*, Giacomo Puccini told the writer of this column that he was "completely charmed by Vienna and by Viennese music." He discovered anew the pure Viennese notes in the dances of Johann Strauss; and Alfred Grünfeld in his inimitable poetic way had to play before the Italian maestro for hours on end [his transcriptions of] Strauss' waltzes.[36] Puccini spent his free evenings in the operetta theater in order to—and at this point a soft laugh came from his lips—"perhaps use that opportunity to make a study on location" for his Viennese opera. We could not believe our ears. True, Richard Strauss in *Der Rosenkavalier* had also paid homage to the Viennese waltz. But Puccini in a Viennese opera? It just didn't seem to make any sense at all. The able manager, Siegmund Eibenschütz, seized upon the idea. Were it not for the intervening world war the Karltheater indeed would have experienced the honor of a Puccini première. . . . It was the first Italian opera to appear in an Austrian publishing house (Eibenschütz & Berté). Thus, everything that was Viennese would be included in the framework of Puccini's new work. Messrs. Willner and Reichert juxtaposed the planned Viennese waltzes of Puccini with a Parisian setting for the scenario. Whether this then conformed with Puccini's wishes remains unclear. One can hardly assume, in view of their literary past, that Paris and the period of the Second Empire were more compatible with their poetic fantasy than Vienna and the time of the modern operetta. In any event, the construction and direction of the action reveal a strong fluctuation on the part of the authors between attraction and talent, between opera and operetta, and only the music allows one ultimately to determine the style and categorization of the work. . . .

Even when reading the libretto one cannot suppress a sigh. More trivial language, more clumsy verses cannot be found in any old opera or any new operetta. As a mitigating factor, we might take into account that the original text had to be translated for the composer, and then retranslated from Italian into German. Therefore, much of the poetic refinement that we automatically would attribute to [Willner and Reichert] may have been lost. But the material itself can hardly be called original; and every attempt at a dramatic formulation, a deeper interpretation, a more gripping characterization is lacking . . . the conflict comes across a bit too threadbare.[37] . . . The heroes of the story are hardly more interesting than the supporting cast. Perhaps Madelaine [Magda]

36. Alfred Grünfeld (1852–1924) was a concert pianist, composer, and arranger, greatly beloved in Vienna. According to the *Neue freie Presse* of 26 October 1913, Grünfeld played for Puccini for three hours at a private gathering ("Puccini findet nicht genug Superlative um Grünfelds poetisches und rhythmisch bezauberndes Spiel zu schildern").

37. The *Neue Musik Zeitung* of 4 November 1920 also blamed the shortcomings of the libretto for the failure of the opera. *Der Merker* objected mostly to the staging.

takes on a touching aspect by her swallowlike longings and quiet renunciation, but we hardly know what to make of the provincial Roger, who interjects himself into a private soiree to convey the greetings of his father, and without saying even a pleasantry to the lady of the house, allows himself to be sent to a night spot by the maid. . . . Puccini's creative musical genius is, however, strong enough to triumph over even a weak libretto. For his beguiling techniques he does not require *Haupt- und Staatsaktion*,[38] large words or pathetic gestures. And if Heine made little *Lieder* out of his terrible suffering, so, too, Puccini has shown us often enough that he is able to create great melody (*Lieder*) from minor suffering. . . . Puccini created a distinctive theatrical technique and handcrafted it with powerful mastery. With Puccini, lyric and drama flow from the same musical source . . . theater music in the good sense, which in sensuous, warm orchestral luster, radiating and infatuating, takes us by surprise—first by its blessed melodious inspiration, then by its refined primitiveness. In addition to the methodically developed mosaic of short recurring motivelike phrases that shine forth and expire, the waltz form prevails in *La Rondine* to a degree that is only found in operettas. Yet even where he descends with lighthearted laughter to Viennese models, Puccini remains—and this cannot be emphasized vigorously enough—he remains a grand master ["ein Grandseigneur"] of ability and taste.

Reitler's article included a review of the open dress rehearsal:

> The Volksoper, whose star was once on the rise with *Tosca*, really needed to use its very best for the première. However, as everyone knows, its director, Weingartner, is conducting in America and his substitute obviously has not been very well chosen. . . . The staging and the direction leave much to be desired and it is painful to have to say that the work probably could have been better presented by any Viennese operetta theater. . . . Conductor Stermich is half-Italian and should therefore be a more convinced and convincing interpreter of the subtle, and always exciting, vibrating orchestral language of Puccini. The leaden boredom on the stage extended itself to the musicians in the pit. Frau [Hedwig] Debicka, an esteemed singer of the Volksoper, is absolutely miscast as Madelaine.[39] Herr [Miguel] Fleta has to learn how to stand and move on the stage. Didn't the director notice at all that this singer in the role of Roger had donned a Pagliaccio mask and steadfastly sang in Italian? A better pair is [Rosa] Wagschal [as Lisette] and [Joseph] Hagen [as Prunier][40]— better voices, a more sensitive presentation. The entire clientele of Le bal Bullier came across as wooden; there was no trace of French elegance and

---

38. A type of comedy performed by wandering entertainers in the seventeenth and eighteenth centuries; probably an indirect reference to *Pagliacci*.

39. Debicka was appearing at the Volksoper *als Gast* (as a guest artist). Stermich and she were husband and wife at the time; she later divorced him. During the 1929–1930 season in Poznan they collaborated on another production of *La Rondine* (in Polish).

40. Hagen made his debut at the Volksoper in 1911–1912. His repertoire included more than seventy leading roles. He became an important baritone in Prague, where he sang, among others, Scarpia (1929), Mozart's Almaviva and Figaro, Posa, Alfio, di Luna, Hans Heiling, and Kothner (in *Die Meistersinger*, under George Szell).

precious little of Puccini's élan. . . . The tremendous success of the opera was predictable. Without question, it is based on Puccini's enormous popularity, a popularity he has enjoyed the world over.

Reitler concluded by comparing *La Rondine* with Mascagni's *Lodoletta* (which means "the little lark"), presented earlier that year at the Volksoper on 9 April: "If the weaknesses of *La Rondine* lead one to assume that this 'Swallow' had not been composed by Puccini, it by far surpasses Mascagni's 'Lark.'[41] With Puccini we are still dealing with a musician of paramount importance who is the leading Italian composer."

The day after the première, Puccini attended a performance of Strauss' *Die Frau ohne Schatten*,[42] and on 14 October he was the guest of honor at a *Festabend* of his music, performed by Lotte Lehmann (whom Puccini considered "a first-class singer"), Fleta, and conductor Stermich. Three days after the concert, Puccini wrote to Sybil Seligman:

> Hotel Bristol
> Vienna
> 17 October 1920

> . . . The *Rondine* went well but I wasn't satisfied with the performance or the *mise-en-scène*. It was given at the Volksoper, and the *Trittico* is coming on next Wednesday at the former Imperial Opera House.[43]

A week later he wrote again to tell her:

> Hotel Bristol
> Vienna
> 25 October 1920

> . . . The newspapers were excellent, but I haven't kept them; that is, I never took the trouble to get them, but just had them translated out loud. . . .
> I can't stand any more of this life—to be truthful, I have had fête upon fête, and these Viennese have no equals in courtesy. . . .
> I am going to rewrite the *Rondine* for the third time! I don't care for this second edition; I prefer the first—the edition of Monte Carlo. But the third will be the first with changes on account of the libretto; Adami has been here and has come to an agreement with the publishers and the Viennese librettists. It appears that next year they will give the *Rondine* at the ex-Imperial Opera House—because this time there was a rather mediocre performance of it at the Volksoper, a theatre of only the second rank.[44]

Little is known about the arrangements for the publication of the Vienna version or about the sources used by the Viennese engravers; however, the score was completely reset in Vienna. So

---

41. On 21 July 1917 this item appeared in *Musical America*: "Italian composers would seem to have been haunting aviaries of late. There are several possibilities left for Leoncavallo and his other colleagues. 'The Crow' or 'The Parrot,' for instance, would be a suggestive title with which to still the clamorings of importunate singers for 'vehicles' for their special powers."

42. In a letter to Riccardo Schnabl, Puccini wrote, "di Wagner non mi importa sono le novità" ("Wagner doesn't matter to me, I am interested in new works"). See Simonetta Puccini, *Giacomo Puccini: lettere a Riccardo Schnabl*, Letter No. 56.

43. Seligman, *Puccini among Friends*, p. 319.

44. Ibid., pp. 319–20. The production at the Staatsoper did not take place.

many factors beyond Puccini's control impeded his efforts to revise *La Rondine*. Carlo Carignani, whom the composer had come to depend on to oversee the preparation of the published versions of his operas and whom he entrusted with the task of making (or refining Puccini's own) piano reductions for the piano-vocal and piano solo scores—including *La Rondine*—died in 1919. Before his death, Carignani was working with Puccini on the *Rondine* revisions. It should also be remembered that Edoardo Sonzogno, the patriarch of the Casa Musicale Sonzogno, died on 14 March 1920, and that Renzo Sonzogno died shortly thereafter, on 2 April 1920 (some sources give 3 April).[45] The administration of the Sonzogno firm was suddenly placed in the hands of members of its board of directors and the lawyer Leopoldo Barduzzi, who is mentioned by Puccini in several letters dating from that time.

PUCCINI'S VIENNESE COLLABORATORS

Sonzogno's Viennese representative, a certain Dr. Pick, presumably played a role in the negotiations for the Volksoper première and in the arrangements for the publication of the Vienna version.

Many commentators have confused Emil Berté (Jr.) (b. 6 December 1898; d. 17 January 1968) with his uncle, the better-known Hungarian composer Heinrich Berté. According to Dr. Karl Eibenschütz, the son of the publisher and impresario Zsigà (Siegmund) Eibenschütz,[46] "Emil Berté was my father's partner on the publishing side." They had their publishing office in the Karltheater, located at Praterstrasse 31. Dr. Eibenschütz has kindly provided the following details:

> Our name is and always has been Eibenschütz and, as such, well known in prewar days and after, as my family, through many of its members in the countries of Austria, Hungary, Germany, Sweden and England, has been much involved and important in the international life of music and arts.
>
> My father, after having studied conducting, piano, violin and composition at the Budapest Conservatorium, moved to Vienna around 1900. A great friend of the house of his parents was Brahms.
>
> My father's first name was Zsigà. As that was too difficult to pronounce in Vienna, he changed his first name after a while into the verbal translation: Siegmund. He died in 1922, sixty-six years of age, born 1856. I remember him as a Hungarian Cavalier in all looks and behaviors—and an outstanding master on the piano. . . . In 1907, my father took over as director of the "Royal and Imperial Privileged" Karltheater in Vienna, buying it in later years with [the profits from] that most successful operetta *Ein Walzertraum*. There followed many years of greatest success, with operettas by Lehár, Kálmán, Strauss and equal composers. . . .
>
> Puccini was, among many other great musicians, a friend of my parents and he came to see my father when in Vienna. At a *Heurigenparty*, as the saying goes, in high spirits, my father suggested to Puccini that he should write once for a change an operetta for the Karltheater, to be published by Eibenschütz & Berté. In consequence, *La Rondine* was created, but found not to be the right thing for our theater, therefore the première . . . took place at the Volksoper.
>
> A very personal memory: after the première, my parents gave a dinner party in our house. As a youngster, but well known to Puccini, I was allowed to be brought in by my governess, to congratulate him. I quite remember his charm

---

45. Edoardo Sonzogno had retired from the firm in 1909 and was succeeded by his son Riccardo. Renzo Sonzogno, Riccardo's cousin, took charge of the administration of the company upon Riccardo's death in 1915.

46. In many sources, Zsigà (Siegmund) Eibenschütz is incorrectly cited as Otto Eisenschitz.

and good looks. He took one of the dinner cards from the table, and wrote on the back the first eight measures of *La Rondine*, dedicated to me by name. I am sorry to say that the card burned with our house, like our theater and manuscripts of Nestroy which were not already stolen, and all papers of Eibenschütz & Berté. Puccini had promised to bequeath the manuscript of *La Rondine* to my father. . . . When my mother tried to get the promised manuscript from Sonzogno, she did not succeed—which was not Puccini's fault.[47]

Dr. Alfred Maria Willner (1858?–1929) was one of the most important Viennese operetta librettists. In collaboration with Heinz Reichert, he fashioned two libretti for Lehár: *Wo die Lerche singt* and *Frasquita*. The latter was freely based on *La femme et le pantin*—a novel by Pierre Louÿs that Puccini had seriously considered setting as an opera. Among Willner's numerous libretti are *Die Göttin von Vernunft* for Johann Strauss; *Der Blizabeiter* (a *Lustspiel* in one act) (with E. Bruell); *Baron Trenck (Der Pandur)* (with Bodansky) for Albini; *Der Eisenhammer* (opera in three acts) for Blagoje Bersa; *Götz von Berlichingen* (a five-act opera, after Goethe) and *Ein Wintermärchen*, both for Karl Goldmark; *Endlich allein* (with Bodansky), *Eva* (with Bodansky), *Der Graf von Luxemburg* (with Bodansky), *Libellentanz* (with Lombardo), and *Zigeunerliebe* (with Bodansky), all for Lehár; *Die Faschingsfee* (with Oesterreicher) for Emmerich Kálmán; *Die grune Katze* (with E. Rubricus); *Die Dollarprinzessin*, *Der heilige Ambrosius*, *Die schöne Risette*, and *Rosen aus Florida*, all for Leo Fall; *Die schöne Saskia* (with Reichert) for Oskar Nedbal; *Ein Ballroman* (with Oesterreicher and Rotter) and *Mitternachtswaltzer* for Robert Stolz; and the famous *Das Dreimäderlhaus* (*Lilac Time*) for Heinrich Berté.

Further examination of two excerpts from the Vienna version of *La Rondine*—the Act I *romanza* and the Act II quartet—prove interesting.

THE ACT I ROMANZA

On 17 September 1918, Puccini wrote from Viareggio to Renzo Sonzogno in Milan:

> Caro Sig. Renzo,
>
> l'accomodo di *Rondine* è ancora un mito! Adami fu qui, ma non potè finire; anzi, per il vero, incominciò la trasformazione ma, giunto allo scoglio, scadeva la licenza e partì con promesse... future. E così ho perduto tre mesi e la *Rondine* è ancora tale e qual era, salvo l'aggiunta dell'aria tenore al primo atto che non si può mettere se non si aggiusta per bene e in meglio il secondo atto nell'incontro dei quattro personaggi avanti il quartetto.

> Dear Mr. Renzo,
>
> The revision of *Rondine* is still a myth! Adami was here, but he was unable to finish; on the contrary, to tell the truth, he began the changes and, just when he came to the hard part, his leave was up [Adami was recalled to arms] and he left with promises . . . for the future. Therefore I lost three months, and *Rondine* is still exactly the same, except for the addition of the tenor's aria in the first act, which cannot be added [to the new edition] in any case until we have fixed, well and for the better, the second-act meeting of the four characters before the quartet.[48]

---

47. Excerpted from a letter from Dr. Karl Eibenschütz (written in English) to Michael Kaye.
48. *Carteggi pucciniani*, Letter No. 732.

Some critics of the Vienna version described Roger's *romanza* as a hymn to Paris in the style of Charpentier's *Louise*; others called it a *Preislied* or a disguised waltz—but then, so is the final trio in *Der Rosenkavalier*. Miguel Fleta managed to turn the Volksoper production into a bilingual pastiche by singing the role of Roger in Italian while the rest of the cast sang in German. (It was a convention of the time that an artist appearing *als Gast* was permitted—but not encouraged—to sing in any language he or she chose, as long as it would show them at their vocal best.)

In the opinion of the Viennese critics, despite some beautiful high notes and sweet pianissimi that he used too often, where vocal technique was concerned Fleta was an unfinished singer. According to Gilda Dalla Rizza:

> I remember one evening in Rome, where, as a spectator, I attended a performance of *Tosca*. With me in the box was my husband and Maestro Puccini; Fleta, "the spinner" ["il filatore"] as Puccini called him, sang the role of Mario Cavaradossi. When the Spanish tenor came to a high note he made the orchestra play softer so that he could spin his long pianissimo. Puccini hated such arbitrary actions, and he became furious when they occurred in his operas. That is just what happened that evening, and how Puccini suffered! After the performance, Fleta had the idea to ask Puccini if he was pleased with his melodious rendition (if he had only known!), and the maestro responded, "Having heard it sung like that, I am ashamed to be the composer." Fleta retorted, "If I had sung it like you wanted it the audience would not have made me repeat the *romanza*." To which, thoroughly annoyed, Puccini replied, "In fact, Caruso had to repeat it three times." The maestro was really angry, and I wanted to vanish underground.[49]

In 1920, Sonzogno published a libretto of the Palermo/Vienna version in Italian only. However, in all of the copies of this libretto that I have examined, the pages that would contain the text of the *romanza* are missing. In German, the text of the *romanza* by Willner and Reichert reads:

Roger
(*in stiller Begeisterung, wie vor sich hin*)

Paris, ja, das ist die Stadt der kühnsten Wünsche, so lang ersehnt, begehrt in Träumen, so wundervoll, leuchtend, lockend!

Du, das Ziel aller Ziele! Du Sirene!

Friedlich verrinnt die Zeit, dämmernd das Leben, wo ich geboren bin, dort ist die Ruhe.

Doch hier umglüht mich ein Zauber so seltsam, der die Sinne berauscht und magisch fesselt.

Hier weht ein Duft wie aus fremden Blütenkelchen! Wie aus verborgnen Tiefen schmeichelnd Stimmen riefen:

Roger
(*in quiet enthusiasm, as if speaking to himself*)

Paris, yes, that is the city of the most extravagant wishes, so long hoped for, desired in dreams, so wonderful, shining, alluring!

Paris, the goal of all goals! You temptress!

Time passes peacefully, life passes into twilight. Where I was born there is peace.

But here a very strange magic is glowing all around me, intoxicating and magically captivating the senses.

Here wafts a fragrance as from strange blossom chalices! As from concealed depths cajoling voices called:

49. Quoted in "Incontro con Gilda Dalla Rizza," Valeria Pedemonte, ed., in *Discotecca alta Fedeltà*, Anno XVI, No. 147, Jan.–Feb. 1975, pp. 32–33.

Ja, als wären erwacht tausend Wünsche, die in mir bisher noch schliefen...

Also: möcht ich gern, da ich ganz fremd mich hier fühle, daß Ihre Güte mich lenkt, daß Sie so gut sind zu sagen, was soll ich! Was beginn ich!

(*Lisette tritt ein mit einem Glas Champagner, das sie auf den Tisch vor Roger stellt. Roger macht ihr ein Zeichen des Dankes, nippt aber kaum. Lisette lächelt und wendet sich zur Gruppe links.*)

Yes, as though a thousand desires, which up to now were asleep within me, were awakened...

Therefore, because I feel so strange here, I would appreciate it if your kindness would guide me and you would be so good as to tell me what I should do! What do I start to do?

(*Lisette enters with a glass of champagne, which she places on the table in front of Roger. Roger gives her a sign of thanks but hardly sips the champagne. Lisette smiles and turns to the group at the left.*)

Adami's Italian text of the *romanza* reads:

Rambaldo

Ed è la prima volta che venite a Parigi?

Ruggero

Parigi! è la città dei desideri*
che s'apre al sogno luminosa di fascini,
di speranze!

È la mèta di tutti! È la sirena!

Dalla semplicità timida e queta
della campagna questo turbamento
prende, trascina in uno smarrimento,
perchè l'anima nostra e onesta e lieta . . .

Qui, tra la folla,
è come camminare fra le dolcezze
dei sognati incanti,

e la pace è travolta nell'ansia nuova
del desiderare.

Ecco: sono qui perchè guidiate il mio
cammino in questa immensa vastità infinita
ch'è luce della vita.

(*Lisette entra e reca una coppa di champagne
che colloca sul tavolo davanti a Ruggero. Questi
fa un cenno di ringraziamento e vi accosta appena
le labbra. Lisette sorride e si avvicina al gruppo
di sinistra.*)

---

*Sonzogno's full score reads: "Parigi! o vastità dei desideri."

LA RONDINE

(Vienna version, 1920)
Act I: Romanza for Tenor
"Paris, ja, das ist die Stadt der kühnsten Wünsche"

German text by
DR. A.M. WILLNER
and HEINZ REICHERT

Music by
GIACOMO PUCCINI
Edited by Michael Kaye

Ru - he. Doch hier um - glüht mich ein Zau - ber so selt - sam, der die

Sin - ne be - rauscht und ma - gisch fes - selt. Hier weht ein

Duft wie aus frem-den Blü - ten - kel - chen!

Wie aus ver-borg-nen Tie - fen schmeich-elnd Stim-men rie - fen: Ja, als wä-ren er -

soll ich! Was be - ginn ich!___

(Lisette tritt ein mit einem Glas Champagner, das sie auf den Tisch vor Roger stellt. Roger macht ihr ein Zeichen des Dankes, nippt aber kaum. Lisette lächelt und wendet sich zur Gruppe links.)

THE ACT II QUARTET

In his letter to Renzo Sonzogno of 8 August 1918, quoted in part on p. 185, Puccini continued outlining the changes he was planning to make in *La Rondine*:

> Aspetto il secondo atto da Adami, poi il terzo, speriamo presto. Sarebbe bene che Carignani venisse qui per mettere in ordine questo primo atto, sia partitura che edizione p[iano] e canto; nel frattempo verrà il secondo atto al quale non ci sono grandi cose da fare; farò un taglio grossetto al valzer per tenere più possibile la folla lontana e lasciar libero il corso alla tenue commedia; poi legherò il quartetto in modo diverso e farò il trasporto d'un mezzo tono del finale.

> I am waiting for the second act from Adami, then the third; let's hope they arrive soon. It would be good if Carignani would come here to put this first act in order, the piano-vocal score as well as the full score; in the meantime, the second act, in which there are not too many things to fix, will arrive; I will make quite a big cut in the waltz in order to keep the chorus as far in the background as possible and leave the way clear for the intimate comedy; then I will [introduce and] set the quartet in a different way and I will make the transposition down one half tone for the finale.[50]

The Act II quartet ranks with the best music Puccini ever wrote. It occurs at the reunion of the principals at the famous Bal Bullier. Magda seeks refuge with Roger to escape the importunity of some unruly students. Prunier, that "prince of poets," and Lisette, a chambermaid modeled after Adele of *Die Fledermaus*, are also present. In the first version of *La Rondine*, the quartet was an integrated ensemble with numerous choral interjections supporting the soloists and filling out the harmonies. In the Vienna version, the chorus has been eliminated and the voicings have been altered, with several lines redistributed among the participants. The entire ensemble was published in Vienna in D-flat major.[51] The introduction has been recomposed: ten measures before rehearsal number 35 have been shortened to six. The alterations in the voice parts begin after Magda's line "Non lo dite, che è troppo imprudente!" and the dialogue leading into the quartet reads:

Lisette
(*umilmente*)
Mi confesso, vedete! . . .
(*Ruggero chiama un cameriere e gli dà ordini a voce bassa. Il cameriere esce.*)
Prunier
(*a Magda*)
Spero sarete pietosa!
Magda
(*completando, ironica*)
. . . Con Salomè o Berenice?
Prunier
Non m'umiliate!

---

50. *Carteggi pucciniani*, Letter No. 726, in which Puccini also stated: "If I don't have some help for the proposed changes and transpositions, I, myself, do not feel capable to do the work well and quickly. As long as Adami doesn't let me down. PS: It would be good if you could write a line of encouragement to Adami."

51. The first edition of the original version (1917) contains an appendix in which the quartet is transposed from E-flat major to D-flat major; this optional transposition begins nine measures before rehearsal number 35. In Sonzogno's "II Edizione" the quartet is also in D-flat major.

Magda
(*ridendo*)
Oramai
L'una e l'altra l'amore legò!
(*Il cameriere reca lo champagne.*)

With the following exceptions, the Italian text of the quartet is virtually identical to the edition of 1917.

Prunier
(*alzando il calice*)
E allora bevo all'amore
che unisce i nostri destini
in un comune giocondo sorriso!

Magda
(*a Ruggero*)
Il mio cuore è conquiso!

Ruggero
(*a Magda*)
T'ho donato il mio cuore!

Prunier
(*a Lisette*)
O mio tenero, dolce mio amore
A te schiude il cammino un poeta!

Ruggero
(*a Magda*)
Fa ch'io viva sempre in te![52]

Dramaturgically, the resulting ensemble is much more intimate.

According to the *Corriere della Sera* of 29 March 1917, the quartet was encored at the Monte Carlo première ("è bissato il Quartetto in mi bemolle"), and at the first performance of *La Rondine* at the Metropolitan Opera, on 10 March 1928, it brought down the house. In his review of the Volksoper production, Josef Reitler wrote: "The champagne inspires Prunier to a melody in D-flat major, which may be considered the single truly sensitive developable melody of the work, and out of which comes a quartet passage full of enchanting warmth and careful construction" (*Neue freie Presse* of 8 October 1920, see above). I hope that its republication in this collection will stimulate interest in performing it.

(*Der Kellner bringt Champagner.*)

Prunier

Weih' ich mein Glas deinem Lächeln, das zart Amoretten umfächeln? Ein Lächeln ist's, das das Leben vergoldet.

Madelaine (*zu Roger*)

Süßer Reiz dieser Stunden!

(*The waiter brings champagne.*)

Prunier

Should I dedicate my glass to your smile, that fans our delicate little Cupid? It's a little smile that is gilding life.

Madelaine (*to Roger*)

Sweet charm of these hours!

---

52. The Italian text is quoted from the 1920 Sonzogno "II Edizione."

202

Roger (*zu Madelaine*)

Tief hab' ich es empfunden.

Prunier

Was ich schwer von der Muse erbeten, schenkt dein Kuß wie von selbst dem Poeten!

Roger (*zu Madelaine*)

Ich will leben dir allein!

Madelaine

Schönster Traum, du wirst jetzt Wahrheit, dunkles Ahnen wird Klarheit! Nie soll der Schimmer verglühen, durchs Leben will ich vereint mit dir ziehen! Nie soll der Duft dieser Liebe entfliehen! Wonnetrunken in Küssen versinken, aus der Quelle der Liebe nur trinken ohne Ende für immerdar!

Roger

Nie soll der Frühling verblühen, nie soll der Schimmer verglühen, durchs Leben will ich vereint mit dir ziehen! Nie soll der Duft dieser Liebe entfliehen! Wonnetrunken in Küssen versinken, aus der Quelle der Liebe nur trinken ohne Ende für immerdar!

Lisette

Wird dir mein Kuß immer neu sein? Wirst du mir treu sein, wirst stets du mir treu sein, sag', sag' mir's, darf ich um dich, ja um dich ranken mich mit zarten Gedanken? Hegst im Busen du die Musen, deine Lieb mir nur gib! Will dein Herz bloß, und nicht zum Scherz bloß! Dein Schatten sein, das sei mein Los!

Prunier

Hörst du die Worte, die süßen, die aus dem Quell meiner Liebe nur fließen? Zart deines Dichter Gedanken wie frische Blüten dich, nur dich umranken! Heg' im Busen ich die Musen, strahlt dein Bild mir doch mild, freundlich blickend, so lockend nickend, und doch dabei voll Schelmerei!

Roger (*to Madelaine*)

I have felt it deeply.

Prunier

What my pleading obtained with difficulty from the Muse, your kiss by itself gives to the poet.

Roger (*to Madelaine*)

I want to live for you alone!

Madelaine

Most beautiful dream, now you become truth, dark forebodings become clearness! Never shall the glimmer lose its glow, I want to go through life united with you! Never shall the fragrance of this love escape! Blissful to sink in kisses, only to drink from the source of love without end forever!

Roger

Never shall the spring fade, never shall the glimmer lose its glow, I want to go through life united with you! Never shall the fragrance of this love escape! Blissful to sink in kisses, only to drink from the source of love without end forever!

Lisette

Will my kiss always be new for you? Will you be true to me? Will you always be true to me? Say it, say it to me. May I be around you, yes around you be with tender thoughts? If you hold the Muses in your bosom, give your love only to me! I want your heart alone, and not merely as a joke! To be your shadow, that should be my fate!

Prunier

Do you hear the words, the sweet ones, which only flow from the source of my love? Your poet's thoughts climb tenderly like fresh blossoms around you, and only you. I hold the Muses in my bosom, but your image appears gently to me, kindly looking, so enticing, winking, and yet full of mischief!

Madelaine

Ja, ach könnte, ach könnte ich hoffen, daß nimmer entschwindet der Schimmer des Glücks, das uns so selig verbunden hat! Geliebter, laß meine Liebe sich entfalten, mit allen Fasern dich zu halten! O nimm mich hin, will nur Dir zart mich neigen, dir zu eigen, nur dein, nur dein! Ja, dann leb' ich in rosigem Schein! Ja, leben, lieben und sterben für dich, dir nur alles, ja alles weih'n!

Roger

Was vordem ich ersehnt, was ich erstrebte, es scheint mir schal, wie verwelkt, grau und fahl, gleich als ob ich nicht lebte, bis eins mich durchbebte: Es war die Liebe zu dir! Nur dir will, nur dir zart mich neigen, dir zu eigen, nur dir, nur dein! Ja, dir ganz mich weih'n! Ja, leben, lieben und sterben für dich, dir nur alles, ja alles weih'n!

Lisette

Wenn du, lorbeerumwunden, dichtest in göttlichen Stunden, vergiß nicht die dein nur denkt und sich ganz dir schenkt! Laß meine Liebe sich entfalten, mit allen Fasern des Herzens immer halten. Eng geschmiegt nur an dich, mit dir mich freu'n, das soll mein Glück sein, dann werd' selig ich sein! Ja, dann leb' ich in rosigem Schein! Ja, leben, lieben und sterben für dich, allein dir nur alles weih'n!

Prunier

Ein Gedicht scheinst du mir reich an reizenden Strophen: Du bist und bleibst doch die Zier; glaub' es mir, die Perle der Zofen, die Perle der Zofen! Du, die ein Dichter besingt, dem doch winkt unsterblicher Ruhm unbedingt! Will dir, nur dir zart mich liebend immer neigen, will dir den Lorbeer ja weih'n! Wirst berühmt durch mich sein! Ja, leben, lieben und sterben für dich, allein dir nur alles weih'n!

Madelaine

Yes, oh could, oh could I hope, that the glow of happiness, which has so heavenly united us, never vanishes! Beloved, let my love unfold, with all its fibre to hold you unto me! Oh, take me, I shall only tenderly bend to you, for you to own me, only yours, yours alone! Yes, then I live in a rosy glow! Yes, to live, to love and to die for you, to dedicate everything, yes, everything to you!

Roger

All that I ever longed for, that which I strived after, seems to be stale, as faded, gray and fallow, as if I did not live, until something made me tremble: it was my love for you! Only to you shall I tenderly bend, for you to own me, only to you, only yours! Yes, to be dedicated to you! Yes, to live, to love and to die for you, to dedicate everything, yes, everything to you!

Lisette

When you, with laurel around you, create poetry in divine hours, don't forget her who only thinks of you and gives her all to you! Let my love unfold to always hold with every fibre of the heart. To cling tightly to you, to be glad with you, that shall be my happiness, then I shall be blessed! Yes, then I live in a rosy glow! Yes, to live, to love and to die for you, only to dedicate everything to you!

Prunier

You appear to me as a poem, rich with charming strophes: you are and will be the ornament; believe me, the pearl of the lady's maids, the pearl of all lady's maids! You, whom a poet extols, you who beckon absolute immortal fame! I shall bend lovingly to you always, yes, I shall dedicate the laurel to you! You will be famous through me! Yes, to live, to love and to die for you, only to dedicate everything to you!

LA RONDINE

(Vienna version, 1920)
Act II: Quartet (S.S.T.B.)
"Weih'ich mein Glas deinem Lächeln"

German text by
DR. A.M. WILLNER
and HEINZ REICHERT

Music by
GIACOMO PUCCINI
Edited by Michael Kaye

* "♩ = 80" in the first version.

206

213

* In the first version (1917), this and the following measure are marked "fff allarg[ando] a tempo con decisione."

214

APPENDICES

Appendix I

Incomplete, Fragmentary, and Missing Songs

"Allor ch'io sarò morto"

Frequently cited as a separate title, these are actually the first words of *Melanconia* (see below).

1881 [?]   MELANCONIA, Romanza

        a) For Baritone and Piano
        b) For Voice and String Orchestra
        Text by Antonio Ghislanzoni

The manuscript, thought to be preserved in the library of the Milan Conservatory, has vanished. According to the late Dr. Karl Gustav Fellerer, the manuscript is dated 19 June 1881. The text was published in Ghislanzoni's *Melodie per Canto* (Milan: Perussia e Quadrio Editori, 1881).

> Allor ch' io sarò morto,
>   I bianchi nidi alla casuccia mia
>   Le rondinelle appenderanno ancor;
> All' alito d' aprile
>   Rifioriran nell' orto
>   Le mammolette e le giunchiglie d ôr.
>
> Di canti e di profumi
>   Si allieterà il mattino,
>   Gli astri raddianti a sera
>   Sfavilleranno nell'azzurro ciel;
>
> E là, fra l'erbe e i dumi,
>   Sotto la croce nera,
>   Sarà eterno il silenzio, eterno il gel.

1882 [?]   AH! SE POTESSE

        For Tenor and Piano

Mario Morini attributes the discovery of this *romanza* to Vittorio Giuliani and reports that the signed four-page manuscript is dated "Lucca 15-7-1882."[1] It was supposedly given to Albina del Panta by her mother, Ramelde Franceschini, the composer's sister. It reputedly begins: "Ah! se potesse / a nuova vita un fiore / rinascer sul suo stelo / e favellar d'amore, / si! quel ch'io feci / ancor faria per te." My efforts to locate the manuscript were to no avail.

---

[1]See Mario Morini's article "Il Puccini Minore" in *Discoteca Alta Fedeltà*, Milan: Anno XVI, No. 147, 1975.

"Spirto gentil"

Frequently cited as a separate title, these are actually the first words of *Ad una morta!* (see below),

---

1882 [?]

AD UNA MORTA!

a) For Baritone and Piano
b) For Baritone and Orchestra
Text by Antonio Ghislanzoni

The earliest extant manuscripts for this work are in the form of sketches for voice and piano. The first is marked "Per Baritono," in E-flat minor (27 measures), 3/4 time; the second consists of 25 measures; and the third comprises a seven-measure fragment for voice and orchestra. These sketches are owned by the Istituto Musicale Pareggiato "L. Boccherini" in Lucca.

Sketch I:*

---

*The musical examples are not intended for performance.

10
c[i]e - li, Spir - to gen - [The text is missing.]
pp
Ped.
13
O-ve t'ag-gi - ri tu? In qual' a-stro ti
16
ce - li? O - ve t'ag - gi - ri tu? Sa - per vor-rei qual
19
si - a La for - ma tua no - vel - la, Sa -

22
per— sein ciel— sei— bel - la
25 Sketch II:
rall.
I° Tempo
29
[The text is missing.]
32

* Measure 24 is a transitional measure found in Sketch I, leading directly to measures 25–34, which are transcribed from Sketch II.

*Measures 35–41 are realized from Sketch III.

Measures 42–44 appear in Sketch II, where they remain unresolved.

Another fragment of the orchestrated version is preserved at the Puccini museum in Celle, located in the province of Lucca in the mountains of the Val di Roggio (Comune di Pescaglia). At least two additional pages in full score and six manuscript pages for voice and piano are suspected to exist. Puccini apparently intended to score the song for 2 Flutes, Oboe, 2 Clarinets, Bassoon, 2 Horns, 2 Trumpets, Trombone, Timpani, Harp, and Strings. He made use of some of the music of *Ad una morta!* in the revised two-act version of *Le Villi*: in No. 9, *Scena Drammatica – Romanza* "Torna ai felici dì," sung by Roberto (tenor) at the words "Ridean i fior, fioria per me l'amor."[2] He further developed other sections of *Ad una morta!* in the *Capriccio sinfonico* (1883) and in *Manon Lescaut* (1893).

Ad una morta! was probably left incomplete. Ghislanzoni's name is written in Puccini's hand at the upper right corner of Sketch I. In the lower right-hand margin Puccini wrote: "seguita in Mi bem[olle] min[ore], poi andare in Mi con o senza pedale doppio per andare in Maggiore compito largo all'orchestra . . . unito al baritono con imitazioni 2ª [volta?]." Sketch I also includes seven measures written out of context and one measure of what appears to be a trial modulation, over which Puccini wrote the words "alla Wagner." (Several years later, in a composition sketch for *Manon Lescaut*, he wrote "Troppo Tannhäuser.")

The complete text of Ghislanzoni's poem as published in *Melodie per Canto* reads:

> Spirto gentil, dal carcere
> Terreno assunto ai cieli,
> In quale astro ti celi?
> Ove ti aggiri tu?
> Saper vorrei qual sia
> La forma tua novella,
> Saper se in ciel sei bella
> Qual eri un dì quaggiù;
> Saper vorrei se gli angeli
> Dell'amor tuo consoli,
> Se pei siderei voli
> I vanni Iddio ti diè.
> Oh! dimmi almen se assorta
> Dei cieli ai gaudii immensi,
> A me talor ripensi
> Com'io ripenso a te!

---

2. According to William Ashbrook, Roberto's aria was completed at San Martino in Colle on 28 October 1884 (Ashbrook, *The Operas of Puccini*, p. 16).

SOLFEGGI
For Voice and Piano

In an article entitled "Unbekannter Puccini," written in 1937 for the *Allgemeine Musikzeitung*, Dr. Karl Gustav Fellerer reports that the manuscript of the *Solfeggi* is dated 20 March 1888 and that the voice part is notated in the treble clef. He also quotes the following incipit as being part of the *Solfeggi:*

Numerous attempts at locating the manuscript of this still unpublished set of vocal exercises have proven unsuccessful. At one time, the manuscript was reportedly on deposit at the library of the Milan Conservatory; the Boccherini Institute in Lucca was also unable to provide any clues as to its whereabouts.

It was certainly not Puccini's usual practice to write pedagogical works. If Fellerer's attribution of 20 March 1888 as the date of composition is correct, then the *Solfeggi* were composed shortly after Puccini wrote *Sole e amore*. It is my conjecture that the *Solfeggi* were written either for a female singer who had engaged Puccini's interest, at the request of a friend, or to generate some much-needed income. Perhaps one day the manuscript will be retrieved from obscurity.

Appendix II
Ditele—A Song Attributed to Puccini

THE SONG *Ditele*, which the majority of discographies ascribe to Puccini, is not by Puccini. Nevertheless, Raffaele Végeto's "Discografia Pucciniana"[1] lists a *romanza* entitled *Ditele*, recorded for the Società Italiana di Fonotipia by the tenor Giuseppe Anselmi (disc number 62186) in "1908 [*sic*]"; Eugenio Gara's "Prospetto cronologico della vita e delle opere di Giacomo Puccini"[2] (among others) corroborates this assertion with the affirmation: "1908—*Ditele*, romanza incisa su disco Fonotipia." This misinformation may have originated with the attribution found in the discography compiled by the famous record collector Roberto Bauer, entitled *The New Catalogue of Historical Records: 1898–1908/09*, which states: "[Fonotipia disc number] 62186—*Ditele*—Puccini."[3]

Franz Pazdírek's *Universal-Handbuch der Musikliteratur aller Völker*[4]—which has a listing for the *Canto d'anime*, the song that Puccini wrote for the Gramophone Company (Italy) Limited in 1904—does not list a published version of a song by Puccini entitled *Ditele*, nor does Hopkinson's bibliography.[5] This omission is not surprising, and the reason for it becomes clear upon an examination of a photograph of the actual Fonotipia record label:

---

1. Published in the *Carteggi pucciniani*.

2. Published in *L'Approdo Musicale* (Rome: ERI, 1959), p. 99.

3. London: Sidgwick & Jackson Ltd., revised edition, 1947, p. 32.

4. Vienna: Pazdírek & Co., 1904–1910.

5. Hopkinson's very informative book, however, fails to include the first edition of *Canto d'anime* in its listing of Puccini's miscellaneous published compositions.

Upon listening to the recording, one discovers a very pleasing salon song, sung by Anselmi in Russian, entitled "скажите ей" ("Skazhite ei," = "Ditele," or "Tell Her"), by the Russian Princess Yelizaveta Vasilevna Kochubei (1822–1897). The Library of Congress owns a copy of this song "translated and adapted from the Russian" as "Did He But Know" (published by Oliver Ditson & Co., Boston, Massachusetts, ca. 1869), which begins:

It is this music that Anselmi sings on Fonotipia disc 62186. (On the reverse side he sings a *romanza* by Karl Youlievitch Davidov [1838–1889] entitled "Kakoe schast'e," or "What Happiness.")

John Reginald Bennett's *Dischi Fonotipia*,[6] presumably based on authentic in-house archival documents of the Fonotipia Company, dates this disc from April 1907 and cites the matrix number 2587 (which corresponds to the one inscribed on the copy of the recording I have examined), and it confirms "[disc number] 62186 Anselmi *Ditele*—Romanza (in russo) Cociubei."

---

6. Published by The Record Collector Shop, Suffolk, England, 1953.

An early Fonotipia brochure published in English and printed in Italy includes the following declaration signed by thirty-one prominent recording artists: "We only recognize as faithful reproductions of our Voice, and as examined and approved of by us, these records which bear our signature. We decline any responsibility for records without our signature, which we give as a guarantee to the public, the publishers and ourselves."

It was not uncommon for the Fonotipia Company to change recorded material from one number to another (including matrix numbers); however, in view of the above, or until information to the contrary surfaces, one can assume that Puccini did not compose a song entitled *Ditele*.

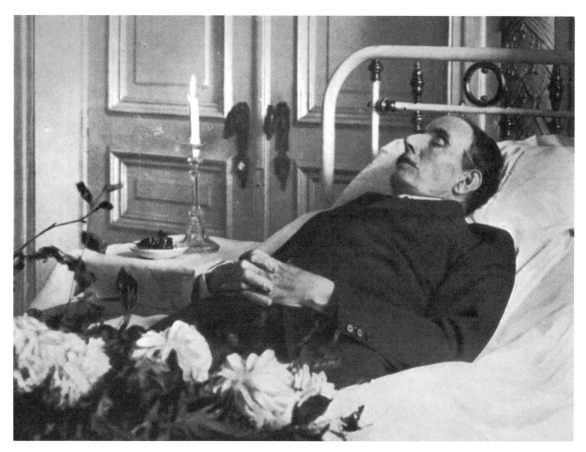

Puccini on his deathbed.

Appendix III
Puccini's *REQUIEM* in Memory of Giuseppe Verdi (1905)

PUCCINI'S *Requiem* for three-part chorus (S. T. B.), solo viola, and organ (or harmonium) was composed in Milan, where it was first performed before a small audience in the chapel of the Casa di Riposo on 27 January 1905 to mark the fourth anniversary of Verdi's death.[1] The *Requiem* was completed on 19 January 1905, only a few days before the première. An account of that event was published in Ricordi's magazine *Musica e Musicisti* on 15 February 1905:

> At 10 A.M. a reverent group of chosen guests convened at the Casa di Riposo. Among them are the president of the Casa di Riposo, Mr. Seletti; the secretary, Mr. Campanari; members of the board of directors, Mr. Ricordi, Mr. Emanuele Greppi, Mr. Piola, and Dr. Bertarelli. Also present are Arrigo Boito; Maestro Puccini and his wife; Lucia Beltrami; Mr. Spatz; Mr. Ajroldi, who represents the mayor; and the families of Ricordi, Origoni, and Mrs. Giuseppina Morisini Prato; and Maestro Gallignani and his wife.
>
> In the Chapel, which is above the tomb of the great Verdi, Don Carlo Mantovani, assistant at San Pietro in Sala, celebrates the Mass while Professor Brognetti plays some of Verdi's most poignant melodies on the harmonium. At the end of the Mass, 30 choristers, chosen from the chorus of La Scala, perform a new *Requiem* by Puccini, who composed it expressly for the occasion.
>
> The voices start in the key of D minor, harmonized with exquisite lightness, while the bass descends in a contrary motion. Very softly, almost breathlessly, the solo viola modulates to the key of A minor, then the voices start again in unison turning toward the plagal cadence, remaining there indefinitely, ethereally suspended on the fourth degree, while the harmonium ends in the tonic of the initial chord.
>
> The very ingenious, surprising conclusion is received by the onlookers with mute admiration—a mute admiration that to Maestro Puccini is worth more than any thunderous applause he could receive in the theater.[2]

The collaborating musicians from La Scala included Professor Pirignoli, solo viola, and Maestro Brognetti, harmonium; the chorus was prepared by Aristide Venturi, who also conducted.

Later in the day, Puccini attended ceremonies held at Brera (in Milan), where sketches for a monument to Verdi were displayed. The memorial tribute culminated at the Regio Conservatorio Giuseppe Verdi with a concert of works by Léo, Vivaldi, Bach, Gluck, Scarlatti, and Viotti.

On 28 January 1973, the *Requiem* was performed at the Church of San Frediano in Lucca. According to Giorgio Magri, who was responsible for rediscovering the work, the autograph manuscript of the *Requiem* (63 measures in all) is in the Casa Ricordi archives, and a copy is preserved at the Museo Teatrale of the Teatro alla Scala. A facsimile of the first page of the manuscript, signed by Puccini and dated 19.1.[19]05, is reproduced in the first edition of the score, edited by Pietro Spada, published in 1976 by Elkan-Vogel, Bryn Mawr, Pennsylvania (plate number 362-03209).

---

1. The Casa di Riposo per i Musicisti, a home for elderly musicians (originally endowed with funding provided by Verdi), is the site of the tombs of Giuseppe and Giuseppina Verdi.
2. Anno 60, Vol. 1, No. 2, pp. 60-II–61-II.

Bibliography

ADAMI, GIUSEPPE. See also Puccini, Giacomo.
————. *Giulio Ricordi e i suoi musicisti*. Milan: Fratelli Treves, 1933.
————. *Puccini*. Milan: Fratelli Treves, 1935.*

ASHBROOK, WILLIAM. *The Operas of Puccini*. New York: Oxford University Press, 1968.

BAUER, ROBERTO. *The New Catalogue of Historical Records: 1898–1908/09*. Rev. ed. London: Sidgwick & Jackson, 1947.

BENNETT, JOHN R. *Melodiya: A Soviet Russian L. P. Discography*. Westport, Conn.: Greenwood Press, 1981.

BOITO, ARRIGO. *Tutti gli scritti*. Edited by Piero Nardi. Milan: Mondadori, 1942.

BONACCORSI, ALFREDO. *Giacomo Puccini e i suoi antenati musicali*. Milan: Curci, 1950.

BUDDEN, JULIAN. *The Operas of Verdi*. 3 vols. New York: Oxford University Press, 1973, 1978, 1981.

CAMBIASI, POMPEO. *La Scala, 1778–1906 note storiche e statistiche*. 5th ed. Milan: G. Ricordi (1907?).

CARDUCCI, GIOSUE. *Poesie di Giosue Carducci: MDCCL–MCM*. 10th ed. Bologna: Nicola Zanichelli, 1927.

CARNER, MOSCO. *Of Men and Music*. London: Joseph Williams, 1944.
————. *Puccini: A Critical Biography*. 2nd ed. New York: Holmes & Meier Publishers, 1974.
————. Introduction to *Letters of Giacomo Puccini*. Rev. ed. Edited by Giuseppe Adami. Translated by Ena Makin. London: George G. Harrap & Co. Ltd., 1974.

CASELLA, ALFREDO. *I segreti della giara*. Florence: Sansoni, 1941.

CASINI, CLAUDIO. *Giacomo Puccini*. Turin: UTET, 1978.

CERESA, ANGELO. See Marchesi, Gustavo.

Critica pucciniana. Lucca: Provincia di Lucca, 1976.

DAVIS, RONALD L. *Opera in Chicago*. New York: Appleton Century, 1966.

DEL BECCARO, FELICE. *Giovanni Pascoli: Lettere agli amici lucchese*. Florence: Felice Le Monnier, 1960.

DEL FIORENTINO, DANTE. *Immortal Bohemian: An Intimate Memoir of Giacomo Puccini*. New York: Prentice Hall, 1952.

DRY, WAKELING. *Giacomo Puccini*. London: John Lane, The Bodley Head, 1906.

FELLERER, KARL GUSTAV. *Giacomo Puccini*. Potsdam: Akademische Verlagsgesellschaft Athenaion, 1937.
————. "Von Puccinis Arbeitsweise," in *Die Musik*, Vol. XXX, July 1937.

FORZANO, GIOVACCHINO. *Come li ho conosciuti*. Turin: ERI, 1957.

FRACCAROLI, ARNALDO. *La vita di Giacomo Puccini*. Milan: Ricordi, 1925, 1930, 1958.

GARA, EUGENIO. See Puccini, Giacomo.

GELATT, ROLAND. *The Fabulous Phonograph: 1877–1977*. 2nd rev. ed. New York: Macmillan Publishing Co., 1977.

---

*First published in 1932 as *Il romanzo della vita di Giacomo Puccini*.

GHISLANZONI, ANTONIO. *Album di romanze per musica.* Lecco: Tip. Vigano, 1877.

———— . *Melodie per Canto.* Milan: Perussia e Quadrio Editori, 1881 (2nd ed. "accresciuta e corretta," Milan: Emilio Quadrio Ed., 1882).

GIOVANNETTI, GUSTAVO. *Giacomo Puccini nei ricordi di un musicista lucchese.* Lucca: Baroni, 1958.

GREENFELD, HOWARD. *Puccini.* New York: G. P. Putnam's Sons, 1980.

GREENFIELD, EDWARD. *Puccini: Keeper of the Seal.* London: Arrow Books, 1958.

HEWITT, VIVIEN ALEXANDRA. "*Le Villi*: avanguardia del post-romanticismo, tra trame, ridde, spettri e amore," in *30° Festival pucciniano*, Summer 1984.

HOPKINSON, CECIL. *A Bibliography of the Works of Giacomo Puccini: 1858–1924.* New York: Broude Brothers Limited, 1968.

KAYE, MICHAEL. "Songs of Puccini." See *The Opera Quarterly.*

LOEWENBERG, ALFRED. *Annals of Opera: 1597–1940.* Totowa, N.J.: Rowman and Littlefield, 1978.

LOMBARDI, IVANO. *Puccini ancora da scoprire.* Lucca: Edizioni Lucensium Civitas, 1976.

MAGRI, GIORGIO. *Puccini e le sue rime.* Milan: Giorgio Borletti Editore, 1974.

MARCHESI, GUSTAVO. *Puccini a casa.* Photographs by Angelo Ceresa. Udine: Magnus Edizioni S.p.A., 1982.

MARCHETTI, ARNALDO. See Puccini, Giacomo.

MARCHETTI, LEOPOLDO, ed. *Puccini nelle immagini.* Milan: Garzanti, 1949.

MAREK, GEORGE R. *Puccini: A Biography.* New York: Simon and Schuster, 1951.

MAROTTI, GUIDO, and PAGNI, FERRUCCIO. *Giacomo Puccini intimo.* Florence: Vallecchi, 1926.

MONALDI, GINO. *Giacomo Puccini e la sua opera.* With a preface by Fausto Salvatori. Rome: Libreria Editrice Mantegazza, 1924.

MOORE, JERROLD NORTHROP. *A Voice in Time: The Gramophone of Fred Gaisberg: 1873–1951.* London: Hamish Hamilton Ltd., 1976.

MORINI, MARIO. *Pietro Mascagni.* Milan: Sonzogno, 1964.

———— . "Il Puccini Minore," in *Discoteca Alta Fedeltà.* Milan: Anno XVI, No. 147, 1975.

Mostra pucciniana (Sept.–Nov. 1974). Lucca: Palazzo Provinciale di Lucca, 1974.

Musica d'oggi: "Questo fascicolo speciale e dedicato alla memoria di Giacomo Puccini" (Anno VII, Supplemento al Numero III). Milan: G. Ricordi e C., 1925.

NICOLODI, FIAMMA. *Gusti e tendenze del novecento musicale in Italia.* With a preface by Fedele d'Amico. Florence: G. C. Sansoni Editore Nuova, 1982.

Opera Quarterly, The. Edited by Irene and Sherwin Sloan. Chapel Hill, N.C.: University of North Carolina Press. Vol. 2, No. 3 (Autumn 1984, Puccini Commemorative Issue) includes "Songs of Puccini" by Michael Kaye and articles by John Ardoin, William Ashbrook, Simonetta Puccini, et al.

PALADINI, CARLO. *Giacomo Puccini: con epistolario inedito,* Edited by Marzia Paladini. Florence: Vallecchi Editore, 1961.

PANCRAZI, PIETRO. "Renato Fucini," in *La Lettura*, 1 April 1921, Anno XXI, No. 4.

PANICHELLI, PIETRO. *Il "Pretino" di Giacomo Puccini.* Pisa: Nistri-Lischi, 1962.

PANZACCHI, ENRICO. *Poesie.* Edited by Giovanni Pascoli. Bologna: Nicola Zanichelli, 1908, 1910.

PICARD, EDMOND. *Étude critique de l'arrêt de la Cour d'Appel de Bruxelles du 29 décembre 1905 en cause de Jules Massenet et Giacono [sic] Puccini.* Brussels: Veuve Ferdinand Larcier, 1906.

PINTORNO, GIUSEPPE. See Puccini, Giacomo, and Puccini, Simonetta.

PINZAUTI, LEONARDO. *Puccini, una vita.* Florence: Vallecchi, 1974.

POMPEI, EDOARDO. *Pietro Mascagni nella vita e nell'arte.* Rome: Tipografia Editrice Nazionale, 1912.

PUCCINI, GIACOMO. *Giacomo Puccini: Epistolario.* Edited by Giuseppe Adami. Milan: Mondadori, 1928.
————. *Carteggi pucciniani.* Edited by Eugenio Gara (with contributions by Mario Morini and Raffaele Végeto). Milan: Ricordi, 1958.
————. *Puccini com'era.* Edited by Arnaldo Marchetti. Milan: Edizioni Curci, 1973.
————. *Puccini: 276 lettere inedite.* Edited by Giuseppe Pintorno. Milan: Nuove Edizioni, 1974.
————. *Giacomo Puccini: lettere a Riccardo Schnabl.* Edited by Simonetta Puccini. Milan: Emme Edizioni S.p.A., 1982.
————. See also Paladini, Carlo.

PUCCINI, SIMONETTA. See also Puccini, Giacomo.
————. ed. (with Giuseppe Pintorno). *Puccini* (catalogue of the exhibition at the Museo Teatrale alla Scala, 30 November 1974–11 January 1975). Milan: Fondazione Museo Teatrale alla Scala, 1974.

PUCCIONI, MARIO. *Cacce e cacciatori di Toscana.* Florence: Vallecchi, 1934.

RICCI, LUIGI. *Puccini interprete di se stesso.* Milan: Ricordi, 1954.

SARTORI, CLAUDIO. *Puccini.* 4th ed. rev. Milan: Edizioni Accademia, 1978.
————. ed. *Symposium 2,* Milan: Ricordi, 1959.

SBROCCHI, LEONARD GREGORY. *Renato Fucini, l'uomo e l'opera.* Florence: G. D'Anna, 1977.

SELIGMAN, VINCENT. *Puccini among Friends.* New York: Macmillan Company, 1938.

SGROI, CARMELO. *Renato Fucini.* Florence: G. C. Sansoni, 1943.

SPECHT, RICHARD. *Giacomo Puccini: The Man, His Life, His Work.* Translated by Catherine Alison Phillips. New York: Alfred A. Knopf, 1933.

TURNER, J. RIGBIE. *Nineteenth-Century Autograph Music Manuscripts in The Pierpont Morgan Library: A Check List.* New York: The Pierpont Morgan Library, 1982.
————. *Four Centuries of Opera: Manuscripts and Printed Editions in The Pierpont Morgan Library.* New York: Dover Publications, 1983.

WEAVER, WILLIAM. *Puccini Librettos in New English Translations.* New York: Anchor Books, 1966.
————. *Puccini: The Man and His Music.* New York: E. P. Dutton, 1977.
————. *The Verdi Companion.* Edited by William Weaver and Martin Chusid. New York: W. W. Norton & Company, Inc., 1979.
————. *The Golden Age of Italian Opera from Rossini to Puccini.* New York: Thames and Hudson, Inc., 1980.
————. "A Puccini Anthology" and "Franco Alfano: Puccini's Posthumous Collaborator," in *Puccini Festival, New York City Opera,* Summer 1983.* New York: New York City Opera, 1983.

Readers interested in the different versions of *La Rondine* might also like to consult the house program of *La Rondine* at the Gran Teatro La Fenice (Christiano Chiarot, ed., Venice: Stamperia di Venezia s.r.l., [May] 1983), which contains some previously unpublished correspondence of Puccini, articles by Fedele D'Amico, Alfredo Mandelli, Elvidio Surian, Angelo Curtolo, and Eduardo Rescigno, as well as the complete text of Sonzogno's three editions of the Italian libretto of the opera.

---

* The festival was canceled due to a labor dispute.

Index of First Lines

General Index